SUGAR AND MODERNITY IN LATIN AMERICA

Interdisciplinary Perspectives

SUGAR AND MODERNITY
IN LATIN AMERICA

Interdisciplinary Perspectives

Edited by

Vinicius Mariano de Carvalho, Susanne Højlund,
Per Bendix Jeppesen, and Karen-Margrethe Simonsen

AARHUS UNIVERSITY PRESS

SUGAR AND MODERNITY IN LATIN AMERICA

© The authors and Aarhus University Press 2014

Layout and typeset: Ryevad Grafisk, Anette Ryevad

Cover design: Jørgen Sparre

The book is typeset in Sabon Lt Std

Production: Narayana Press, Gylling, Denmark

Printed in Denmark 2013

ISBN 978 87 7124 110 5

Aarhus University Press

www.unipress.dk

The publication of this book was made possible by a grant from
Aarhus University Research Foundation.

Content

PART FOUR:
THE ART OF SLAVERY

Foreword

In the last 15 years, type 2 diabetes has spread with frightening speed all over the globe. Latin America is no exception; it has witnessed an explosion of cases of diabetes, especially in Brazil and Mexico. An increase in diabetes is often accompanied by an increase in obesity in the population, and it seems to follow the spread of so-called modern lifestyles which include a relatively large sugar intake. However, the relationships between diabetes, sugar intake, and the significant factors of a modern lifestyle are rarely investigated and documented, and when they are, the cultural and historical contexts of particular lifestyles are often not considered. Likewise, the approach to sugar and health problems often represents a specific but unexamined approach to modernity.

The basic idea of this book is twofold and interdisciplinary: the first assumption is that it is impossible to understand the growth of diabetes without investigating and understanding modern lifestyle(s) in their cultural contexts. It is implied here that modernity, despite its proclaimed uniformity and global spread, acts in different ways, according to local traditions. Therefore it is not enough to diagnose the problem of diabetes and its possible relation to specific eating habits; we also have to understand the cultural contexts of these habits. Assuming that sugar plays a significant role in relation to modern lifestyle diseases, we have to ask ourselves how sugar intake occurs in different cultures, whether there is cultural diversity in the sensory perception of sweetness, and whether there are historical reasons why sugar plays such a huge role in certain cultures and not in others. In order to answer these questions, we have to use humanistic approaches to help clarify the importance of cultural contexts for the development of unhealthy lifestyles, and consequently, the development of conditions like diabetes.

The second assumption is that sugar production and sugar cultures are closely related to a specific historical period of modernity, and that studying sugar production and sugar cultures in a cultural context helps not only to qualify, but also to question and reflect critically on the concept of modernity. Understanding the concept of modernity requires us to look deeper into history and into cultural products such as religion and literature, as well as the popular conceptions reflected in advertising. In these cultural expressions, sugar's modern and anti-modern aspects are negotiated in the most dynamic and unforeseen ways, making it the ideal locus for a more nuanced approach to the understanding of modernity.

The aim of this book is thus to contribute both to the understanding of the cultural contexts for the development of 'dangerous' lifestyles and to a critical understanding of the concept of modernity. In other words, the book analyzes the relation between diabetes and modern sugar cultures, as well as the ways in which specific sugar cultures and cultural expressions about sugar raise serious questions about our understanding of modernity.

Latin America is an especially interesting place for this investigation, since sugar as a product and sugar production have played a vital role in the modern development of many countries in the region, for instance Mexico, Cuba, Brazil, and Bolivia – all of which will be studied in specific detail in this volume. Sugar cane is not native to Latin America. It was imported to the continent after Columbus's conquest in 1492, but sugar production developed quickly with the help of European know-how and machinery and African slaves. The largest plantation areas of sugar cane today are still in Latin America; the region is the biggest producer of sugar in the world; its colonial and modern history can be read parallel to the history of the sugar (plantation, production, and consumption); and social and health problems associated with sugar are also bigger in Latin America. Yet Latin America is not one culture. As mentioned above, we will focus specifically on Mexico, Cuba, Brazil, and Bolivia, bringing together countries that are often studied separately in Spanish/Latin American studies, Brazilian studies, and Caribbean studies. Our objective is to allow for a comparative approach and a transnational Latin American understanding.

Sugar production in general is often seen as the catalyst of modernity, but because of the hierarchical, paternalistic power structure and the use of force on sugar plantations, it also came to represent the darker side of modernity. Many theorists have described Latin American development as uneven and contradictory. It is both modern and anti-modern, and it both renews and retrieves at the same time. Thus ancient and even pre-Columbian traditions live side by side with extreme technological modernization and many new cultural products mix old and new influences in unforeseen ways. As Fernando Ortiz pointed out in 1940 about the context of Cuba, it is a culture of simultaneity of cultures that derive from different historical origins and a mestizo culture that mixes different cultural and racial traditions. Despite national differences, Latin America is impregnated with such a mestizo culture. One is thus constantly forced to rethink current ideas about modernity. And as was argued by Ortiz and more recently by the anthropologist Peter Wade, we should understand not only that Latin America is a product of mixed heritage but also that European heritage is itself mixed and that Latin America has always been constitutive of European modernity. Latin America has functioned not only as a 'black' mirror-image but as a real political and cultural influence. European economic and cultural development depends on the traditions and products of Latin America.

Sugar is an especially interesting product since it incarnates both tradition and modernity and shows many of the dynamic interactions between Europe and Latin America at political, economic, cultural, and medical levels. In the 21st century, this interaction has become even more visible, as Latin America slowly becomes a dominant world power in politics and economy, but it is also visible in medicine: one of the new plants that may help diminish rates of diabetes derives from Latin America, namely from Paraguay where it has been cultivated by the Indians for centuries. Stevia has turned out to be a 'miracle' plant, in the sense that it produces 'sugar' many times sweeter than normal sugar that does not cause the same health problems as normal sugar. Stevia has recently been used by Coca-Cola to produce a healthier version of the drink; some scientists are calling it the second sugar revolution.

In this book, modernity is thus not a set term. We hope to challenge and discuss what it means while focusing specifically on sugar in different contexts. A mixture of different cultures and social habits influence sugar cultures and specific understandings of sugar, including its cultural and symbolic value, its taste and its use in different cultural and religious contexts, and even its methods of production. Of course we are talking about the same 'sugar', that perhaps should be more properly called 'sucrose' or 'sacharose', an organic compound extracted from the sugar cane (Saccharum officinarum L.) represented by the molecular form $C_{12}H_{22}O_{11}$. However, every time we hear or use the word 'sugar' we can realize the powerful polysemy of it. Thousands of associations are triggered by the word: health, nutrition, diet, poverty, sweetness, honey, good taste, slave labour, commodity, and money to name only a few. Sugar was once associated with social prestige, but today a large sugar intake is associated with underdevelopment and a lower social class. Changes in the symbolic value of sugar can be analyzed through literature or through anthropological or sociological fieldwork.

Throughout this book, sugar functions as a prism for understanding the complicated relations between disease and cultural and social habits, between past and present, and between symbolic meanings and material effects. Since the book's ambition is to connect the how and the why of diabetes, sugar culture, and modernity, we have chosen an interdisciplinary approach. It is not possible to answer our question about sugar cultures from a single perspective, of hard science or of anthropology, for example. In the book we have chosen a far wider interdisciplinary approach. Here you will find approaches by experts in medical science, agriculture, sociology, and anthropology, as well as Latin American, Brazilian, and literary studies. This scope is unusual but we believe that interdisciplinary dialogue is necessary to qualify questions about modernity in depth. Since modernity is not only a philosophical idea or a term for a period of technological or economic advance but also a concept that includes a complex understanding of cultural identity and symbolic value, it cannot be studied by one or two disciplines alone. Similarly, any attempt to understand the relation between a disease and its triggers in cultural patterns and historical traditions demands an interdisciplinary research method. Grand challenges need interdisciplinary approaches.

However, interdisciplinary work itself always comes with its own challenges, for instance in terms of methodology and consistency of vocabulary. Although concepts travel between disciplines, they often tend to mean different things in different disciplines – even within the humanities. There is thus an acute epistemological challenge in interdisciplinarity that cannot easily be done away with. In fact, according to our experience, good interdisciplinary collaboration acknowledges that this challenge cannot be eliminated and maybe also that it should not – but neither should it be ignored. We do not offer our reader any consensus on the subject of modernity or sugar, but rather a work in which each contribution is highly aware of the interdisciplinary dialogue of which it is part. We have chosen to let the methodological approach of the book be plural, but all its chapters address the same basic questions; it thus presents the result of truly collaborative learning.

The book is divided into four parts that each focuses on a special perspective on sugar and modernity. It is introduced by Jim Mann, Professor of

Human Nutrition and Medicine at the University of Otago, and Director of the Edgar National Centre for Diabetes and Obesity Research (ENCDOR) and the WHO Collaborating Centre for Human Nutrition.

In the first section, we focus on the Problem of Health and raise the question of whether there is a correlation between modern lifestyles that imply higher sugar consumption and the increased health problems in Latin America. The chapter by Per Bendix Jeppesen has a medical approach but at the end he also suggests that the consequences of high sugar intakes may be reduced by introducing stevia in food production. Stevia has been proven to decrease the postprandial blood glucose level in human beings as well as the total energy intake; this is one of the reasons why the production of stevia has been called the second sugar revolution.

In the second part, we discuss the preference for sweetness both from a physical and an anthropological point of view. Ulla Kidmose and Heidi Kildegaard describe how scientific tests have shown that the sense of sweetness varies not only according to age and gender but also to eating habits. In an anthropological study in Cuba, Susanne Højlund shows how eating sugar to a large degree is dependent on cultural traditions, local conditions, and history. But she also demonstrates that the case of Cuba raises some serious questions regarding the relation between sugar intake and disease, because in 1991 Cuba consumed the most sugar per capita of any nation in the world and at the same time experienced a decrease in the so-called lifestyle diseases. This example challenges the hypothesis of a direct connection between sugar consumption and such diseases.

In the third part we focus on what we call glocalized practices of sugar, that is, the relationship between local and global traditions in sugar cultures. From a sociological point of view, Ken Henriksen analyzes the curious blend of local religious traditions and modern capitalistic systems in Chamula in Mexico, where Coca-Cola is used in Christian services. The article also analyzes the way Coca-Cola brands itself as an ethical and responsible company in an advertisement directed at the Latin American market. Annie Oehlerich discusses the use of sugar and sweetened products in old Quechua rituals in which sweetness is associated with Mother Earth. She also describes how these old rituals have had a renaissance since modern politicians have begun paying tribute to them to show themselves as sympathetic to indigenous traditions. The actualization of these sugar rites is an example of the way old and new are mixed in Latin American culture. In this section's final chapter Gitte K. Bjoern and Ulla Kidmose study the modernity of cultivating methods, looking back to older traditions and forward to how sugar production methods will develop. These production methods are again influenced both by local traditions and the global market and technology.

The final part of this book is concerned with the darkest side of sugar production, namely the history of slavery. We have called it "The Art of Slavery" since its focus is on literature. Vinicius Mariano de Carvalho discusses the perception of modernity in the Brazilian writer José Lins do Rego's sugar cane cycle, which gives a vivid depiction of life on the sugar plantations from the early period when its family mode and pre-modern power structures were intact until modern urbanization disrupted the life of the plantations and turned them into "factories." Carvalho argues that the cycle of novels should not only be seen as a nostalgic chronicle of plantation life but as a critical reflection on the sugar plantation, since the protagonist is not a former slave or son of slaves but sugar itself as a social catalyst. In the final chapter Karen-Margrethe Simonsen discusses how the sugar culture in Cuba has intermingled with transcultural images of national identity, analyzing how the grim history of slave labour is being remembered and transformed in the poetry of Nicolás Guillén. It is argued that sugar in Guillén's poetry constantly appears as a doubly coded symbol of the gruesome destiny of the slave and the positive and multicultural coherence of Cuban identity.

All sections begin with opening remarks that introduce more general perspectives than the individual chapters themselves give, forming links between their approaches.

This book has been written by researchers in the group SUMOLA (Sugar and Modernity in Latin America), all attached to Aarhus University. It is the fruit of many interdisciplinary discussions, and it is our hope that because of its interdisciplinary scope, it can help establish new truths and ask new questions about the relation between lifestyle diseases, modernity, and sugar.

We would like to thank Aarhus University Science Foundation for their support of this book. Without it, publication would not have been possible.

Sweet reading!

The editors
Aarhus 2013

Introduction

By Jim Mann

Sugar has for centuries had a profound influence on food choice, food preservation, culture, politics, trade, the economy of food-producing countries, and even literature. Sugar has for some been a useful source of cheap calories but for others, when consumed in excess, it is a potential threat to human health. Nowhere are these consequences of cultivation and consumption of sugar more important than in Latin America. In the early 16th century, the Portuguese recognized the potential for growing sugar cane in Brazil. Sugar cane plantations and mills soon appeared and with the ready availability of slave labour, a lucrative export industry developed for the colonists. This book describes, through a series of essays, some aspects of the influence that the cultivation and consumption of sugar has had in Latin America – a region that produces and consumes a significant proportion of the world's supply of sugar.

Given the recent interest in sugar and human health it is not surprising that the first chapter in the collection and several others are directed at the effects of sugar on human health. When considering the relevant scientific literature, it is important to remember that the term 'sugar' is used to refer to sucrose produced from sugar cane or sugar beet, whereas today caloric sweeteners in the food supply include several other sugars, including high fructose corn syrup. The association between dental caries and sugar, especially when consumed in large amounts and between main meals, is well established, but the extent to which sugar consumption contributes to the major chronic diseases including coronary heart disease, type 2 diabetes, and cancer, remains a subject of debate. However, from a practical perspective the issue has been largely resolved in that sugar (in sugar-sweetened beverages and foods) has been clearly established as a contributor to the obesity epidemic.[1] Obesity is a major determinant of type 2 diabetes and an important risk factor for coronary heart disease and some important cancers (large bowel cancer and postmenopausal breast cancer), thus at the very least sugar can be regarded as an indirect driver of these important chronic diseases as well as the other consequences of obesity. Whether sugar does have some uniquely adverse effect on metabolism and whether other sugars in the food supply, such as high fructose corn syrup have a similar effect remain the topics for further research. The evidence against high fructose corn syrup and fructose itself is steadily accumulating. Given that Brazil has the largest production of sugar worldwide and that Brazilians have the highest per capita consumption of sugar (nearly 60kg per annum), the situation is particularly alarming here, but these issues are certainly not confined to Brazil. The fact that in Cuba the increased rate of obesity and non-communicable diseases has not been paralleled by an increase in sugar consumption does not exonerate sugar as an important cause of obesity and its co-morbidities. There are many interrelated causes which cannot be disentangled by simply examining population trends.

The extent to which sugar-sweetened beverages have pervaded the social fabric of Latin America is well illustrated by the chapter describing the role of Coca-Cola in Mexico. Not only is the beverage marketed (and widely con-sumed) alongside a company campaign promoting "living positively" which includes the promotion of sports, it has even found its way into the religious rituals of remote areas of the country. A scene is described in which Cola is to be found alongside candles, eggs, and a live sacrificial chicken as part of a healing service in a local church. The drink is considered sacred and included in such rituals to make people burp. Total consumption of the beverage is high despite high rates of malnutrition. A different but relevant further illustration of the importance of sugar in the Latin American context is the symbolism of sugar amongst the highland Indians of Bolivia. Mother Earth is considered to have a sweet tooth and sugar forms an essential component of sacrificial rituals aimed at ensuring a good harvest. Sugar even has an established role in literature. In the final chapter, we learn how the history of sugar has found its way into the poetry of Cuba.

---

[1]   Te Morenga, L., Mallard, S., & Mann, J. (2013). Dietary sugars and body weight: Systematic review and meta-analyses of randomised controlled trials and cohort studies. *BMJ*, vol. 346, p e7492. doi: 10.1136/bmj.e7492.

Clearly action is needed in terms of a raft of measures to stem the tide of the obesity epidemic and chronic diseases associated with it in Latin America and worldwide. Reducing intake of sugar is one such option, but it will certainly not be easy in Latin America, given the entrenched role of sugar in many of the societies in that part of the world. Whether non-caloric sweeteners derived from the stevia plant, native to South America, will prove to be the new "sugar revolution", as Per Bendix Jeppesen has opined, remains to be seen. In the interim, this book provides stimulating reading and an indication of the challenges ahead.

PART ONE: THE PROBLEM OF HEALTH

Opening Remarks

By Per Bendix Jeppesen

I often ask myself what makes Latin America Latin America. All my life I have been attracted to this continent, even before I ever visited it. An old Brazilian saying states "God is Brazilian; he created Brazil first, then paradise." Thus even in paradise you will find that things do not always appear as they really are. The Latin American countries still have major economic and social problems – it counts among the countries with the world's most uneven wealth distributions – however, these figures are changing rapidly. In 2011, Brazil reached its lowest level of wealth concentration since 1960. Between 2000 and 2010, the average income shot up 20 percent in some parts of the country. Infant mortality dropped nearly 50 percent and life expectancy went up from 70 years, in 1999, to 73 in 2009.

The reason for the rapid transition this region has undergone is thought to lie in the exertion of many processes of modernization on Brazil throughout its history. These processes are thought to have been set in motion with the arrival of Christopher Columbus in 1492. Not only was Christopher Columbus responsible for the change of the landscape of the Americas, partly due to sugar cane and coffee bean production as well as to gold mining, but he also introduced new cultures and habits. For example, the western impact on Brazilian food and culture is very apparent. This is important because the identity of a country or region is strongly based on the food it eats. A good illustration of the close relationship between food and culture is the concept of the New Nordic Kitchen, which has its own border, identity, and personality. Diners frequenting the New Nordic Kitchen can literally incorporate elements of another culture into their body and consciousness. You eat, so to speak, into a unique piece of Scandinavia. The New Nordic Kitchen has a strong focus on the importance of the Nordic *terroir* in the development of unique Nordic ingredients. Before anything else, the New Nordic Kitchen meets the modern man's need to feel like a unique individual. It occurred as a response to a cultural transition, i.e. in a time when major changes in everyday life have meant that time, space, and social relations gradually split up, and when you no longer are born with a fixed identity linked to gender, class, or profession.

It is perhaps the case that the same mechanism took place in Latin America during the onset of the modernization process introduced by Christopher Columbus to "the new world." After such a revolution, the individual must seek to create an identity to structure a meaningful life. Here, food often plays a major role as a practical way of expressing certain norms and values. New food ingredients were introduced to Latin America during the creation of "the new world," including sugar from sugar cane, which have now been integrated into the Latin American diet and culture. Interestingly, in many ways Latin American cuisine and diet is founded on adaptive processes like the Acaraje' from Africa and the Pastel of Hispanic or Portuguese origin. The Brazilian "sweet tooth" was developed through the influence of the Europeans, and especially the Portuguese, who brought their sugar and many sweets with them to be used in desserts and other dishes. These cultural changes in food consumption that carry with them a high sugar content may be the reason for the epidemic increase in welfare diseases in this region. This is thought to be a consequence of modernization processes transforming Brazil from an agricultural into an industrial society. The adoption and integration of high calorie sweetened Latin American food is not just a question of health and physiology, but also one of social and cultural aspects. The following chapter attempts to visualize how the region's culturally determined high intake of cane sugar may affect the health of its societies.

CHAPTER I

Is There a Correlation Between High Sugar Consumption and the Increase in Health Problems in Latin America?

By Per Bendix Jeppesen

The United Nations has recently declared that, for the first time in human history, chronic non-communicable diseases such as heart disease, cancer, and diabetes pose a greater health burden worldwide than infectious diseases, contributing to 35 million deaths annually. This problem is not limited to the developed world. The rapid processes of modernization in Latin American countries are adding new challenges to the old and well-known social, economic, and health problems.

One issue is the rapid demographic and nutritional transition that Latin America has undergone over recent decades. The majority of the Latin American population has changed its diet and physical activity patterns to fit an industrialized country model, consequently increasing the prevalence of lifestyle diseases. The incidence of type 2 diabetes (T2D) and metabolic syndrome (MeS)[1] has escalated to epidemic proportions worldwide, and many causes, including dietary components, have been suggested. Excessive calorie intake has been related to high-fat foods and increased portion sizes, but particle diets high in simple sugars may also play a critical role in the epidemic of obesity, T2D, and cardiovascular diseases, which together we call the MeS. Despite a reduction in fat intake in the last decade, the obesity epidemic has continued to rise. Due to this paradox the focus has now shifted. Fructose in particular is now believed to play a critical role in the epidemic of welfare diseases as

---

[1]   Metabolic Syndrome is a combination of the medical disorders that, when occurring together, increase the risk of developing cardiovascular disease and diabetes to diets and products high in simple sugars such as sucrose and high-fructose corn syrup (HFCS).

sugar consumption has increased dramatically over the last few centuries due to greater availability and price decline. The average sugar intake per capita was about 1.8 kg/year in the 18th century; it has now reached about 70 kg/year. Such a dramatic change in sugar intake obviously affects our health and physiology negatively, causing an increased economic burden on society. We know that Latin American countries are the biggest producers of sugar globally, the world's largest exporters of sugar cane, and among the world's largest consumers of sugar per capita. In this regard, it is interesting to observe that the diet consumed by the aboriginal populations in Latin America has a much higher diversity of food components than the food we consume in the modern western world. Beside describing an urgent need to alter our intake of sugars or to find alternative consumer accepted calorie reduced sugars to fructose, sucrose, and glucose in our food products, a second aim of this paper is to try to outline any evident correlation between high sugar consumption and the increased health problems seen in Latin America in particular.

SUGAR INTAKE

While today the intake of foods containing table sugar (sucrose) occurs with almost every meal, the introduction of refined sugar into the diet as an organoleptic and preservative substance is relatively recent.[2] Before the 15th century sugar was a profitable luxury only a few could afford, mainly royalty or the very wealthy (Galloway 1989). The primary sweetener had been honey, but since it was relatively rare and not mass produced, the majority of people (and especially the poorer classes) had no sweeteners at all in their everyday diet (Sheridan 1973). The typical diet consisted mainly of carbohydrates, primarily starch from barley, wheat, oats, and rye (Sheridan 1973). Interestingly we know that the diet of the aboriginal populations in Latin America is much more diverse and contains a much higher amount of health promoting nutrients e.g. secondary metabolites. Later, after Christopher Columbus had brought cane sugar to grow in "the new world" on his second voyage, it became an important ingredient in our diets. Sugar cultivation was labour intensive and created a market for a slave trade. Although an initial attempt was made to use Native Americans as labourers on the plantations, it was the more than 10-20 million enslaved Africans, forcibly removed to Latin America, that promoted the

---

2   High-fructose corn syrup comprises a group of corn syrups that has undergone enzymatic processing to convert some of its glucose into fructose to produce a desired sweetness.

intensive cultivation of sugar (Deer 1950). From a human health perspective, it is important to clarify that sugar intake should be divided into two main types: the intake of "intrinsic" sugars integrated within intact fruits and vegetables, and the intake of saccharides that are added to foods and drinks by food producers (added sugar). Dietary guidelines do not recommend restriction in terms of intrinsic sugars or milk sugars (lactose and galactose) since these are not believed to cause adverse health effects at the present time.

As sugar production and availability increased its price declined, which lead to a dramatic increase in sugar consumption. The average per capita sugar intake was about 4 lb (1.8 kg/year) in the 18th century and 18 lb (8.1 kg/year) in the 19th; it increased even more after the English prime minister William Gladstone removed the sugar tax in 1874, which led to a mean consumption of 100 lb (45 kg/year) in 1950 (see Fig. 1) (Deer 1950, 2003; Johnson et al. 2006, 2009).

By the early 1970s, an additional sweetener called high-fructose corn syrup (HFCS) had appeared on the market. It had certain advantages over table sugar as regards shelf life and cost. This HFCS sweetener is similar to that of disaccharide sucrose as they both contain glucose and fructose,[3] but

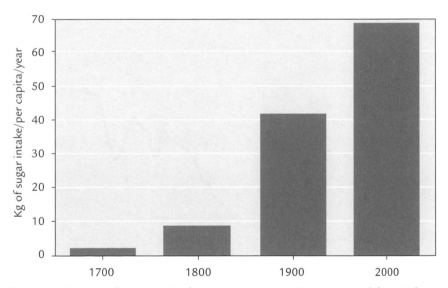

Figure 1. Sugar intake per capita from 1700 to 2007. Data extracted from Johnson et al, 2006; 2009.

---

3   A disaccharide is a carbohydrate formed when two monosaccharides undergo a condensation reaction.

HFCS appears as monosaccharides, and is used extensively to sweeten soft drinks, fruit juice, and other processed foods. The combination of table sugar and HFCS has resulted in an additional 30% increase in overall sweetener consumption over the past 40 years, mainly in soft drinks (Deer 2003; Johnson et al. 2006, 2009). Currently, consumption of these sweeteners stands at about 150 lb (67.6 kg) per person per year (see Fig. 1) (Deer 2003; Johnson et al.2006, 2009,). Today more than 50 percent of all Americans consume 180 lb per year (81 kg) (Lustig 2012).

It may be obvious to everyone that this kind of extreme change in diet over the last few centuries may negatively affect our health and physiology. There are some striking epidemiologic correlations between sugar intake and the epidemic of lifestyle diseases, as obesity was initially seen primarily in the wealthy, who were the first to be able to afford sugar. Interestingly, the first documentation of hypertension, diabetes, and obesity occurred in the countries (England, France, and Germany) where sugar first became available to the

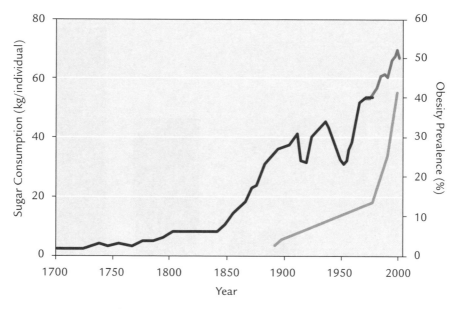

Figure 2. Sugar intake per capita in the United Kingdom from 1700 to 1972 (Deer 1950; Yudkin 1972) and in the United States from 1972 to 2000 (Hallfrisch 1990) is compared with obesity rates in the United States in non-Hispanic white men aged between 60-69 (Helmchen 2004 et al.).

public. The rise in sugar intake in the UK and the USA also correlates with the rise in obesity rates observed in these countries (see Fig. 2).

Furthermore, the introduction of sugar in developing countries also correlates with the rise in their incidences of obesity and lifestyle diseases. A series of epidemiologic studies linked the consumption of soft drinks to obesity, hypertension, and diabetes and the consumption of fruit juice and fruit punch to obesity in children (Sharman 2004 et al.; Bray 2010). Several FAO/WHO reports have also confirmed a link between intake of sugars and chronic disease. However, the FAO/WHO reports recognize that there may not be a direct causal association between the consumption of sugar and coronary heart diseases;[4] they recognize that sugars contribute to energy density in a diet, and thereby indirectly to the global epidemic of obesity which we know is a risk factor for lifestyle diseases such as type 2 diabetes and coronary heart disease. In many parts of the world, people are consuming an average of more than 500 calories per day from added sugar alone (see Fig. 3).

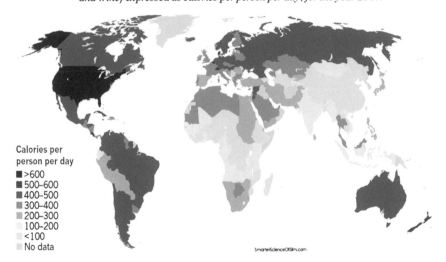

THE GLOBAL SUGAR GLUT

Global sugar supply (in the form of sugar and sugar crops, excluding fruit and wine) expressed as calories per person per day, for the year 2007.

Calories per person per day
- >600
- 500–600
- 400–500
- 300–400
- 200–300
- 100–200
- <100
- No data

SmarterScienceOfSlim.com

Figure 3. The Global Sugar Glut. From Nature, 2012, based on data from Lustig, 2012.

---

4   Coronary artery disease (CAD) is the most common type of heart disease and cause of heart attacks.

On the other hand many epidemiological studies show a potential causal role for high sugar intake, but are there any direct experimental data to show that sucrose or fructose can induce obesity, diabetes, and hypertension? This question will be my focus for the rest of this article.

What about Latin America? We know that the biggest country in Latin America, Brazil, is not only the world's biggest producer of sugar in the world, but also one of its biggest consumers of sugar (see Figs. 4a and 4b). In 2007, per capita sugar consumption was highest in Cuba, followed by Australia and then Brazil, although a substantial portion of Brazilian sugar was converted into ethanol for transportation fuel (Koo et al. 2013). Per capita sugar consumption in the United States was 32 kg, which was above the world average, but for the United States we have to take into account the consumption of HFCS, which makes it the biggest consumer of simple sugar in the world. Of the countries for which data existed, China had the lowest per capita sugar consumption at 7 kg per capita, a figure that is expected to increase substantially as the country's per capita income increases. Annual global sugar consumption for the 2007-2011 periods was 154 million metric tons (Koo et al. 2013).

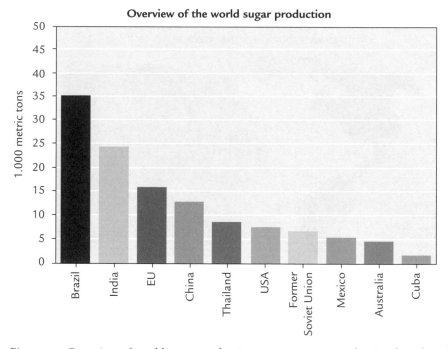

Figure 4a. Overview of world sugar production: average sugar production for selected countries in the period 2007-2011. Data extracted from Koo et al. 2013.

Latin America encompasses 21 countries and a total population of about 500 million; the populations in individual countries are made up of varying proportions of Native Americans and other ethnic groups. The frequency of diabetes in any given country is affected by its ethnic composition as well as by its degree of urbanization and the life expectancy of its population. A study of seven Latin American and Caribbean cities, coordinated by the Pan American Health Organization (PAHO) in 2000-2001, found that 45% to 72% of adults aged 60 and older in those cities had an elevated body mass index (Grupo de investigacion de la Red Qualidiab 2001). The prevalence of arterial hypertension ranged from 44% to 54%, and of diabetes from 13% to 22%. These conditions affect people from both high and low socioeconomic backgrounds. A study in Peru, for example, found little difference between upper and lower socioeconomic groups in terms of the prevalence of hypertension and obesity (Grupo de investigacion de la Red Qualidiab 2001). The report from PAHO 2001 highlighted the major problems in the poorer,

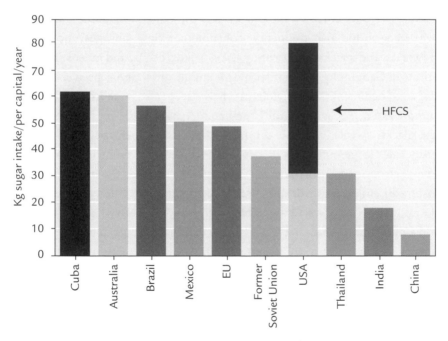

Figure 4b. Consumption of sugar per year per capita. Average sugar consumption for selected countries in the period 2007-2011. Data extracted from Koo et al. 2013. NB: The data only demonstrate the consumption of sugar from sugar beet or cane; it does not include sugar from other sources such as HFCS, which is widely used in the USA. The red lane indicates the intake of HFCS in USA.

marginally employed population, where minimal treatment of diabetes alone (not considering any complications or commonly co-morbid conditions), was estimated to cost between 650 US$ and 1200 US$ yearly, equal to about 50% to 90% of the participants' annual income. Interventions were initiated to improve diet with an increased intake of fibre and legumes and a lower intake of fats. The project was well received but ineffective as the population was forced to purchase whatever food was least expensive and most filling, as many families had to choose between buying medicine, buying healthy food, and paying their utility bills.

In the biggest and most developed country in Latin America, Brazil, the average diet combines the traditional rice and beans with food containing few nutrients and a lot of calories. The daily ingestion of fruits, vegetables, and greens is below the levels recommended by the Ministry of Health (400g) for more than 90% of the population. Conversely, consumption of beverages with added sugar (juices, fruits drinks, and soft drinks) is double that of the recommended average. This statistic is mostly due to Brazil's teenagers, who consume twice as much of these drinks as the country's adults and elderly. This demographic also frequently consume cookies, sausages, mortadella, sandwiches, and snacks, while eating fewer salads, beans, and greens (Brazilian Institute of Geography and Statistical Communication). It has been shown that some components of a healthy diet, such as rice, beans, fresh fish, and cassava flour, are eaten less as the family income increases, to be replaced by pizza, fried snacks, sweets, and soft drinks. In Brazil's rural districts, the average diet includes large quantities of rice, beans, fish, sweet potato, cassava flour, and mango, among other things. In urban areas, however, the most frequently consumed items are soft drinks, bread, beer, pizza, and filled cookies. These data and others were made available by the study "Analysis of the personal Food Consumption in Brazil", which was conducted in partnership with the Ministry of Health in a publication of the 2008-2009 Consumer Expenditure Survey (POF) (Brazilian Institute of Geography and Statistical Communication 2009, 2011). For this study, data about individual food digestion were collected from residents aged 10 or over, distributed across the 13,569 households selected from the original sample of the 2008-2009 POF, which covered 55,970 households (Brazilian Institute of Geography and Statistical Communication).

As we know that physical activity is very important in relation to controlling diabetes, it is interesting to read in the report from Grupo de investigacion de la Red Qualidiab, that there seems to be some barriers to increasing physical activity, including a lack of comfortable, safe places to even take a walk. High summer temperatures and high levels of crime in poor neighbourhoods prompted participants to stay inside and pass their free time watching television (Grupo de investigacion de la Red Qualidiab). Another alarming fact is that the prevalence of T2D and other lifestyles diseases is much higher in urban areas. The frequency of diabetes in Latin America is expected to increase by 38% in urban population over the next 10 years, compared with an estimated 14% increase in the total population. The total number of cases of diabetes is expected to exceed the number of cases in the US, Canada, and Europe by 2025 (Grupo de investigacion de la Red Qualidiab 2001). Factors underlying this increase include the aging and increased life expectancy of the population, increased urbanization, and lifestyle changes among Native American populations. In many places, only a minority of individuals currently receive treatment for diabetes in Latin America. Furthermore, the diagnosis of T2D often occurs late in the course of the disease, with the result that 10-40% of patients have chronic complications at the time of diagnosis. Hospital costs account for the most direct expenditures associated with treatment, and mortality associated with diabetes has increased markedly in some areas over the past two decades.

HOW DOES HIGH SUGAR CONSUMPTION CAUSE INCREASED HEALTH PROBLEMS?

The ability to use a food source for energy is critical to the success of any species, and nature therefore has very sophisticated mechanisms to regulate this process. Such mechanisms are extremely complex; only those mechanisms that relate to T2D will be summarized here, for the sake of simplicity.

The last three decades have witnessed an inexorable rise in obesity, diabetes, and metabolic syndrome coincident with a rise in daily calorie intake (Centers for Disease Control). Quantitative overconsumption of various macronutrients has been postulated to contribute to metabolic syndrome (Zivkovic et al. 2007). Some suggest that specific dietary fats, such as saturated and trans fats, are the culprits (Verna et al. 2008). In October 2011, the Danish government chose to tax foods high in fat, but most medical professionals no longer believe that fat is the primary culprit as the absolute consumption of dietary fat has not changed in the last 30 years (Chanmugam et al. 2003). The tax was abolished in January 2013, following massive protest from the food industry.

Another likely culprit is monosaccharide fructose. In 2002, Havel's group (Elliott et al. 2002) made the conclusion that the fructose content of sugar may be the critical component associated with the risk of obesity and therefore also diabetes. Sucrose is a disaccharide consisting of 50% fructose and 50% glucose; HFCS is also a mixture of free fructose and glucose but contains a higher fructose content (Jurgens et al. 2005; Fig. 5). An ever-increasing proportion of calories in the US diet are derived from fructose. Before 1900, the US population consumed approximately 15g of fructose a day (4% of total calories), mainly through fruit and vegetables. In the 1930s, fructose intake had increased to 24g/day; by 1977, 37g/day (7% of total calories); by 1994, 55g/day (10% of total calories); and current estimates put fructose consumption by adolescents at 73g/day (12% of total calories) (Vos et al. 2008). As seen from the data, fructose consumption has incrementally increased fivefold in the last century and doubled in the last 30 years. In the past, fructose was in fact proposed as the ideal sweetener for people with diabetes because of its inability to raise serum glucose levels and its insulin-independent metabolism. Many investigators have elaborated on fructose's unique hepatic properties and have indirectly implicated fructose in the dual epidemics of obesity and T2D, as well as giving it primacy in the pathogenesis of metabolic syndrome. The Danish government is now considering taxing sugar as well – a more

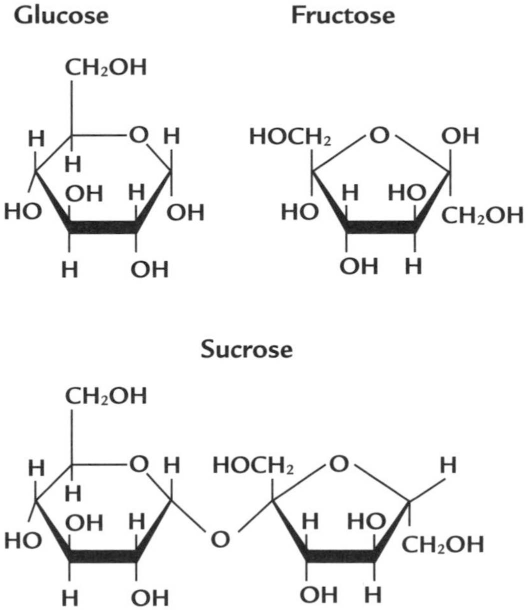

Figure 5. Structures of HFCS and sucrose. High fructose corn syrup is 42-55% fructose; sucrose is 59% fructose.

plausible and defensible step, especially if added sugar is defined as any sweetener containing the molecule fructose that is added to food in processing. The American Heart Association has also recently called for a reduction in added sugar intake to help quell these epidemics (Johnson et al. 2009).

The digestive and absorptive processes for glucose and fructose are different. When disaccharides such as sucrose or maltose enter the intestine, they are cleaved by disaccharidases as the enzyme sucrase catalyzes the hydrolysis of sucrose to fructose and glucose. A sodium-glucose co-transporter absorbs the glucose that is formed during the cleavage of sucrose. Fructose, in contrast, is absorbed further down in the duodenum and jejunum by a non-sodium-dependent process. Although the intestine and kidney possess the Glut5 transporter to reabsorb fructose into the bloodstream, only the liver possesses the Glut5 fructose transporter to metabolize fructose (Lustig 2010). Following the ingestion of 120 kcal of sucrose, for example 8 oz (237 ml) of orange juice, which is composed of 60 kcal fructose and 60 kcal glucose, the overwhelming majority of the 60 kcal fructose bolus reaches the liver, along with 20% of the glucose bolus (12 kcal), making a total of 72 kcal; thus, the liver must handle triple the substrate as if it were glucose alone (Bizeau et al. 2005). After absorption, glucose and fructose enter the portal circulation and are either transported to the liver, where the fructose can be taken up and converted to glucose, or passed into the general circulation. The addition of small, catalytic amounts of fructose to orally ingested glucose increase hepatic glycogen synthesis in human subjects and reduces glycemic responses in subjects with T2D (Petersen et al. 2001), which suggests the importance of fructose in modulating metabolism in the liver. This beneficial effect is however only applicable in a hypocaloric (e.g. starvation) state, in contrast to a hypercaloric state, where fructose drives *de novo lipogenesis* (DNL) (the conversion of fructose into fat),[5] resulting in dyslipidemia, steatosis, and insulin resistance akin to that seen with ethanol (alcohol) (Fig. 6).

When fructose is metabolized in the liver, it is converted into fructose-1-phosphate by the enzyme fructokinase. The reaction is an adenosine triphosphate-requiring reaction, which leads to the depletion of intracellular phosphate and promotes other enzymatic reactions which increase the formation of uric acid (Taylor E N. Et al. 2008).

---

5   *De novo lipogenesis* is the process by which acetyl-CoA is converted into fatty acids.

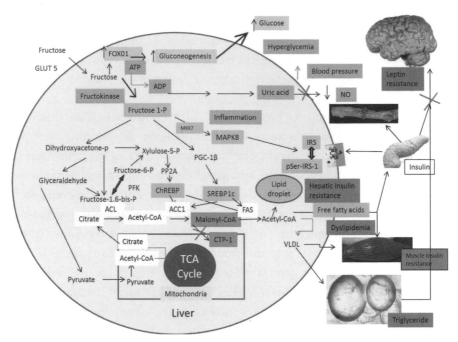

Figure 6. Hepatic fructose metabolism. Of an ingested sucrose load, 20% of the glucose and 100% of the fructose is metabolized by the liver. Fructose induces sub-strate-dependent phosphate depletion, which increases uric acid and contributes to hypertension through inhibition of endo-thelial nitric oxide synthase and reduction of nitric oxide (NO); de novo lipogenesis (DNL) and dyslipidemia; hepatic lipid droplet formation and steatosis; muscle insulin resistance; c-jun N-terminal kinase (JNK-1) activation, contributing to hepatic insulin resistance, which promotes hyperinsulinemia and influences substrate deposition into fat; increased forkhead protein-1 (Foxo1), promoting gluconeogenesis and hyperglycemia; and central nervous system (CNS) hyper-insulinemia, which antagonizes central leptin signaling and promotes continued energy intake (Vos et al. 2008).

Increased concentration of uric acid in the circulation inhibits endothelial nitric oxide synthase, resulting in decreased nitric oxide in the vasculature (Taylor et al. 2008). Nitric oxide is an endogenous vascular smooth muscle relaxant; its depletion by urate results in hypertension (Nakagawa et al. 2006a) (Fig. 6). Recently, sugar consumption has been correlated with uric acid concentrations in adult populations (Gao et al. 2007). Similarly, in the recent National Health and Nutrition Examination Survey evaluation, soft drink consumption in adolescents demonstrates a positive relationship with uric acid levels and with systolic hypertension (Nguyen et al. 2009).

The fructose load converted to fructose-1-phosphate in the liver enters the Embden-Meyerhoff glycolytic cascade, where fructose-1-phosphate is metabolized to pyruvate, which contributes to a large volume of acetyl-CoA entering the mitochondrial TCA. The liver mitochondria are not able to metabolize all the produced pyruvate/acetyl-CoA substrate, so some will be released as citrate to the cytoplasma via the citrate shuttle (Fig. 6). Another product of this process is xylulose-5-phophate, a potent stimulator of protein phosphatase 2A, which activates the carbohydrate response element-binding protein, stimulating the activity of all three DNL enzymes – adenosine triphosphate citrate lyase, acetyl-CoA carboxylase, and fatty acid synthase – which then rebuild the excess cytoplasmic citrate into fatty acyl-CoA and free fatty acids (Dentin et al. 2006) (Fig. 6). Furthermore, fructose also stimulates a transcriptional coactivator for the enzyme SREBP-1c, which further accentuates DNL enzymatic activity (Nagai et al., 2009). The increased DNL results in dyslipidemia, hepatic lipid deposition, and inflammation.

Furthermore, the hepatic insulin resistance induced by fructose due to increased lipid deposition results in gluconeogenesis, contributing to hyperglycemia and increased beta-cell insulin strain. In particular, fructose recapitulates the pentad of metabolic syndrome and has been shown to contribute to cardiovascular disease (Fung et al. 2009). Lustig et al. (2010) detect similarities between the intake of fructose and ethanol as they are congruent evolutionarily and biochemically. Ethanol is manufactured by the fermentation of fructose; the only difference between them is that for fructose, humans perform the glycolysis, while in the case of ethanol, yeast organisms have already performed the glycolysis (Lustig et al. 2012). Secondly, through their free reactive carbonyl moieties, both fructose and ethanol produce Reactive oxygen species (ROS) which increases the risk of hepatocellular damage (Lustig et al. 2012). Table 1 illustrates how fructose can trigger processes that lead to liver toxicity and a host of other chronic diseases. While a small intake of fructose and sucrose is not a problem, excessive consumption induces all of the diseases associated with metabolic syndrome.

Another relevant phenomenon concerns the effect of fructose on insulin release. Along with 2 peptides, glucose-dependent insulinotropic polypeptide and glucagon-like peptide-1 (both released from the gastrointestinal tract), circulating glucose increases insulin release from the pancreas (Edwards et al. 1999). Fructose does not stimulate insulin secretion in vitro, probably because the beta cells of the pancreas lack the fructose transporter Glut-5. Thus,

Chronic ethanol exposure	Chronic fructose exposure
Hematological disorders	
Electrolyte abnormalities	
Hypertension	Hypertension (uric acid)
Cardiac dilation	
Cardiomyopathy	Myocardial infarction (dyslipidemia, insulin resistance)
Dyslipidemia	Dyslipidemia (de novo lipogenesis)
Pancreatitis	Pancreatitis (hypertriglyceridemia)
Obesity (insulin resistance)	Obesity (insulin resistance)
Malnutrition	Malnutrition (obesity)
Hepatic dysfunction (alcoholic steato-hepatitis)	Hepatic dysfunction (non-alcoholic steatohepatitis)
Fetal alcohol syndrome	
Addiction	Habituation, possible addiction

Table 1. Comparison of health problems caused by excessive consumption of alcohol and fructose.

when fructose is given in vitro as part of mixed meal, the increase in glucose and insulin is much smaller than when a similar amount of glucose is given. Insulin release can modulate food intake by at least 2 mechanisms. Schwartz et al. (1989) have argued that insulin concentration in the central nervous system has a direct inhibitory effect on food intake. In addition, insulin may modify food intake by its effect on leptin secretion, which is mainly regulated by insulin induced changes in glucose metabolism in fat cells (Havel 2002). Insulin increases leptin release with a time delay of several hours. Thus, a low insulin concentration after ingestion of fructose would be associated with a lower average leptin[6] concentration than would be seen after ingestion of glucose. Because leptin inhibits food intake, the lower leptin concentrations induced by fructose would tend to enhance food intake. This is most dramatically illustrated in humans who lack leptin becoming extremely obese

---

6   Leptin is a weightregulating hormone that develops in tissues of fat.

(Saad et al. 1998). The low leptin concentrations that occur alongside a high fructose intake are associated with increased hunger and gains in body fat. To the extent that fructose increases in the diet, one might expect less insulin secretion and thus less leptin release and a reduction in the inhibitory effect of leptin on food intake, i.e., an increase in food intake.

Many studies document that increased administration of sucrose supplements results in weight gain, a significant rise in serum triacylglycerols, and a rise in systolic blood pressure (Saad et al. 1998). A study recent published by Richensen's group clearly demonstrates the potential effect of consumption of sucrose-sweetened soft drinks (SSSDs) on human health (Maersk et al. 2012). A total of 47 subjects were randomly assigned 4 different test drinks, and required to drink 1 litre a day for a 6-month period: an SSSD (regular cola), isocaloric semiskim milk, an aspartame-sweetened diet soft drink, and water. The relative changes between baseline and the end of the 6-month intervention were significantly higher in the regular cola group than in the 3 other groups for liver fat (132-143%, sex-adjusted mean; o<0.01), skeletal muscle fat (117-221%; p<0.05), visceral fat (24-31%; p<0.05), blood triglyserides (32%; p<0.01), and total cholesterol (11%; p<0.01) (Maersk et al. 2012) (see Fig. 7). The conclusion of the study was that a daily intake of SSSDs increases ectopic fat accumulation and concentrations of triglyceride and total cholesterol compared with other drinks, and is likely to enhance the risk of cardio-vascular and metabolic diseases (Maersk et al. 2012). The authors suggest that if you want to improve the health of the population, the intake of SSSDs should be reduced considerably.

An increase in blood pressure was also observed in healthy adults fed a diet of 33% sucrose for 6 weeks (Israel et al.1998). Others have also reported that diets enriched in either sucrose or fructose cause impaired glucose tolerance and insulin resistance (Cohen et al. 1966). Notably, most of these diets provided fructose in the range of 400-800 kcal/day, which is within the upper range of what is currently being ingested in many countries around the world. Rodents also develop features of metabolic syndrome after ingesting sucrose. As in humans, it was shown that the active ingredient is fructose rather than glucose: feeding fructose to rats resulted in metabolic syndrome, whereas equivalent amounts of glucose or starch did not induce these features (Nakagawaet al. 2006b).

Figure 7. The figure shows the relative changes in ectopic fat accumulation in visceral adipose tissue (VAT), liver, and skeletal muscle. Forty-seven volunteers drank 1 litre of 1 of 4 test drinks daily for 6 months: regular cola (n=10), milk (n=12), diet cola (n=12), or water (n=13). A) VAT was measured by MR imaging. B) Liver fat and C) skeletal muscle fat were determinated by 1H-MR-spectroscopy. Data was sex-adjusted for the mean relative changes from baseline to 6-month levels and were compared with a general linear model of univariate ANOVA; P<0.05 (Maersk et al. 2012).

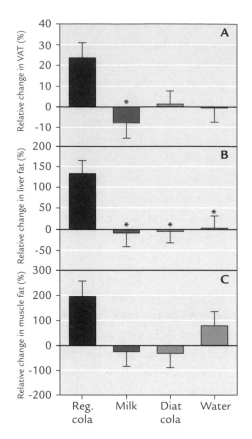

WHAT CAN LATIN AMERICA DO TO REDUCE CONSUMPTION OF SUGAR?

From the scientific literature there is no doubt that the rise of obesity and T2D parallels the increase in sugar consumption, especially in the form of sugar-sweetened soft drinks (Bray et al. 2004). Sugar-sweetened soft drinks contribute 7.1% of an average total energy intake and represent the largest single food source of calories in most diets in the region. Based on the WHO data, the Brazilian Food Guide recommends a dietary sugar intake that provides no more than 10% of energy intake (EI) (Nishida et al. 2004). Latin America is the world's largest producer of sugar cane but few surveys have been published on dietary sugar intake. The 2008/9 household budget surveys for Brazil showed that consumption of sugars remained at 16.4% of energy intake over the past five years. The maximum of 10% of energy intake from sugars is largely exceeded by people belonging to all socioeconomic levels (Brazilian Institute of Geography and Statistics 2009, 2011).

A recently published Brazilian study focused on primary dietary sources and factors associated with the excessive intake of added sugar among adults and elderly in the biggest city in Brazil, Sao Paulo, demonstrated clearly that soft drinks were the main source of added sugar among adults, while table sugar was the main source of added sugar among the elderly. Soft drinks and table sugar accounted for more than 50% of the sugar consumed (Bueno et al. 2012). A Brazilian study also indicated that soft drink consumption (in grams) was higher among men and twice as high among adults compared to the elderly; however, women have more diversified added sugar intake that includes chocolate, cakes, and industrialized juices (Brazilian Institute of Geography and Statistics 2009, 2011). Changing the average intake of soft drinks is thus one option for reducing overall consumption of sugar. Several studies have found an association between sugar-sweetened beverages and incidence of obesity in children (Ludwig et al. 2001). In one study, the odds ratio of becoming obese increased 1.6 times for each additional sugar-sweetened drink consumed every day (Ludwig et al. 2001). This means that consuming one 12- oz can of sugar-sweetened soda per day, containing 150kcal and 40-50g of sugar, as part of a typical diet and after offsetting against a reduction in other caloric sources, may lead to a 15lb (6.75kg) weight gain in one year.

From a public policy perspective, the extant data should help to redefine guidelines for sugar consumption, especially as regards soft drinks and fruit juice products. Producers in Latin America tend to add extra sugar to freshly pressed juice products, which increases level of plasma TG due to the synergistic effect created when glucose is combined with the high content of fructose in the juice (Hudgins et al. 2011). One mechanism that potentially contributes to this effect is a more rapid and complete gastrointestinal absorption of fructose when ingested with glucose (Truswell et al. 1988; Choi et al. 2003; Ravich et al. 1983; Kneepkens et al. 1984; Rasmussen et al. 1986). Governments should support local efforts to banish soda machines from schools or replace soft drinks with healthier options (e.g. unsweetened fruit drinks). A recent randomized clinical trial has shown that a targeted, school-based intervention resulting in a modest reduction in the number of carbonated drinks consumed succeeded in reducing weight problems among children (James et al. 2004). Another method would be to find a non-caloric sweetener as a replacement for sugar, but there are already growing concerns about the effects of high-intensity sweeteners such as cyclamate and saccharin.

One of the solutions for this worldwide burden of growing rates of lifestyle diseases may come from Latin America, in the form of the non-caloric sweetener compound discovered in the plant *Stevia rebaudiana*, which has been used among the Guarani Indians in Paraguay and Brazil for centuries to sweeten their *mate* tea (Bertoni 1899). The two sweetener compounds in the plant stevia are stevioside and rebaudioside A. It was approved by the US Food and Drug Administration in 2008, which listed the product as "generally recognized as safe" (GRAS) for human consumption as a general purpose sweetener. Europe approved the sweetener in November 2011.

STEVIA: THE SECOND SUGAR REVOLUTION

The discovery of stevia sweeteners has been designated as a second sugar revolution. Steviol glucoside is a natural sweetener extracted from the stevia plant that may be able to halt the increase in incidences of MeS, due to its non-caloric content. However, data from human intervention studies on health effects and knowledge about sensory perception of sweetness, food technological aspects, and consumer preference are lacking as regards foods and diets sweetened with this stevia compound.

The South American stevia plant contains non-caloric sweetener compounds and has been used by Guarani and Ache Indians in Paraguay and Brazil for centuries, particularly to sweeten their *mate* tea (a kind of herbal tea). Besides using stevia leaves to sweeten their tea, the Indians also consider it to be a medicinal plant and use it to treat the symptoms of T2D and hypertension. Stevia was first described by the Paraguayan botanist Moises Santiago Bertoni back in 1899, after he learned about the plant's unique characteristics from the local Guarani Indians (Bertoni 1899). The plant contains many different compounds. The two best known are stevioside and rebaudioside A, which are respectively 300 and 450 times sweeter than sucrose (table sugar). Stevia sweeteners have been used successfully for over 30 years in Japan, which approved stevia as a sweetener ingredient as early as 1985 (Buyse et al. 2004). Many other governments followed suit, including the US, Israel, Switzerland, China, and now finally the EU. Japan is by far the leading country with regard to the use of stevia as a sweetener. Forty-one percent of all added sweeteners used in Japan are currently derived from the stevia plant. It is interesting that Japan's population has one of the lowest incidences of obesity: less than 5% are obese compared with nearly 35% in the US (World Health Statistics; data used is from 2008). Whether this can be directly related to the country's greater use of stevia is not currently documented. We also know that the Japanese do not snack like Americans do; although there are vending machines everywhere in Japan, very few of them sell snacks or soft drinks – they are full of unsweetened tea and coffee beverages for the most part. Unsweetened green tea is especially popular, more so than soft drinks.

One of the new interesting sweetener is rebaudioside A (Reb A), extracted from the stevia plant with very environmentally friendly methods, using predominantly water and alcohol. However, it is a fact that human intervention studies on health-promoting effects are inadequate when we talk about diets and foods sweetened with Reb A.

In a collaboration between Aalborg University and the University of Aarhus, researchers carried out tests in 2008 on a small population of T2D subjects. A postprandial meal test was used to see how blood glucose levels are affected by the stevia sweeteners (mixture of stevioside / rebaudioside A (STM)) (Andersen et al., 2008). The pilot clinical study used a blind crossover method that included four men and two women, all with well-regulated T2D. In the experiment, stevia sweetener was used to replace sugar and was taken with a standard breakfast. The only difference between the two meals consumed by the participants was that the 170 grams of freshly squeezed grapefruit juice was sweetened with either 55 grams of sucrose or 0.15 grams of stevia sweetener. The total energy was calculated to be 1114 kJ for the meal sweetened with stevia and 2048 kJ for the meal containing sugar. Accordingly, the substitution reduced the calorie content by 84%, although only a small portion of the meal was changed, namely, the grapefruit juice. The relative difference calculated for the two meals was 156% (Fig. 1 A, B). This means that the post-prandial blood glucose (IAUC) of the participants who consumed the stevia sweetener was 156 percent less than the IAUC of those in the sugar group.

This small study showed that one can achieve better glycemic control through the substitution of sugar with stevia sweetener. A sensory test using the Visual Analogue Scale form also demonstrated that participants preferred the taste of stevia as a sweetener to the real sugar. There is no doubt that these data will be significant for T2D and obese individuals; it seems that stevia will be able to help them achieve healthy blood glucose levels and therefore reduce diabetic complications and maintain a negative or neutral energy balance in order to prevent weight gain (Andersen et al. 2008).

Turning to the physiological action of stevia sweeteners, we know that they are capable of affecting the endocrine system e.g. by simulating insulin secretion, like glucose (Jeppesen et al. 2000; Jeppesen et al. 2002; Jeppesen et al. 2003; Abudula et al. 2004; Hong et al. 2005; Dyrskog et al. 2005;

A

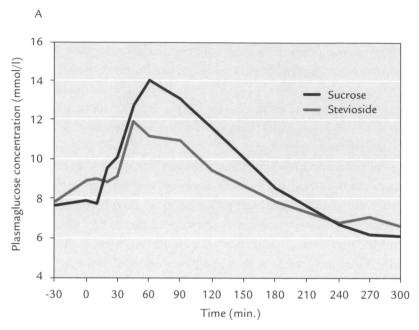

Figure 8A. *Postprandial blood glucose response after the two STMs. Data points are given as mean ± SEM.*

B

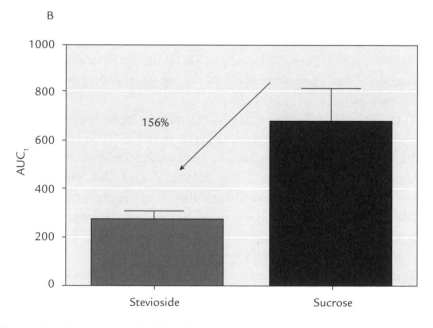

Figure 8B. *Mean postprandial blood glucose AUC_i ± SEM for the two STMs.*

Chen et al. 2006; Hong et al. 2006; Jeppesen et al. 2006; Chen et al. 2007; Nordentoft et al. 2008; Abudula et al. 2008; Chen et al. 2012). As described below, fructose does not stimulate insulin secretion in vitro, probably because the beta cells of the pancreas lack the fructose transporter Glut-5, and since sucrose contains about 50% fructose, this may have an important influence as we know insulin release can modulate food intake both via the central nervous system and via leptin secretion, which has a direct inhibitory effect on food intake (Schwarz et al. 1989). Thus, a low insulin concentration after ingestion of sugars with high fructose content would be associated with lower average leptin concentration than would be seen after ingestion of glucose and possibly stevia sweeteners (the latter's effects on leptin release have not been investigated until recently). The increased level of plasma leptin concentrations induced by glucose and perhaps by stevia sweeteners would be expected to result in less hunger and less weight gain, which may be the key to solving the epidemic of MeS and obesity.

The serious metabolic complications that increasingly plague overweight children and adults include dyslipidemia, fatty liver, and insulin resistance, which may promote cardiovascular disease and diabetes. One dietary pattern that may worsen the complications of obesity is excessive consumption of sugar. One possible explanation for this connection is the stimulation of hepatic synthesis of the saturated fatty acid palmitate, and the secretion of palmitate-enrichedtriglyceride (TG) in very low-density lipoprotein (VLDL) (Chen et al. 2012; Parks et al. 2000; Hudgins et al. 2000).[7] This process, known as *de novo* lipogenesis (DNL), occurs after the flux of glucose and/or fructose through the glycolytic and lipogenic pathways in the liver. DNL is most potently stimulated by dietary fructose, which, unlike glucose, increases hepatic DNL within hours (Hudgins et al. 1996 and 1998; Parks et al. 2008). Careful evaluation of the lipogenic effects of fructose is important because evidence is mounting that increased hepatic DNL causes dyslipidemia, fatty liver, and insulin resistance (Chong et al. 2007; Stanhope et al. 2008; Johnson et al. 2009; Bray et al. 2010; Petersen et al. 2007). Our current knowledge about the metabolism of stevia sweeteners indicates that they do not affect DNL; this is yet another thing in their favour.

In conclusion, current research demonstrates that stevia sweeteners as a substitute for sucrose decrease postprandial blood glucose levels in T2D

---

7   Very low-density lipoprotein (VLDL) is a lipoprotein made by the liver that enables fats and cholesterol to move within the water-based solution of the bloodstream.

subjects as well as their total energy intake. Stevia sweeteners such as rebaudioside A are promising new products that may bring huge benefits to people suffering from obesity and T2D. If stevia sweeteners are capable of changing the world's enormous sugar intake and thereby improving health conditions, they have a right to be described as a new sugar revolution!

BIBLIOGRAPHY

Abudula, R., Matchkov, V.V., Jeppesen, P.B., Nilsson, H., Aalkjær, C., & Hermansen, K. (2008). Rebaudioside A directly stimulates insulin secretion from pancreatic beta cells: a glucose-dependent action via inhibition of ATP-sensitive K+-channels. *Diabetes, Obesity and Metabolism*, vol. 10, pp. 1074-1085.

Andersen, C.A., Kristensen, C.M., Jensen, L., Andersen, M.B., Linemann, T., Larsen, T., Jardin, K.G., & Jeppesen, P.B. (2008). Stevia og type 2 diabetes. *Medicin med Industriel specialisering*, Aalborg University.

Bertoni, M.S. (1899). El Caa-e-he (Eupatorium rebaudianum, especias novas). Rev. Agr. Asuncion, vol. 1, pp. 35-37.

Bizeau, M.E., & Pagliassotti, M.J. (2005). Hepatic adaptations to sucrose and fructose. *Metabolism*, vol. 54, pp. 1189-1201.

Bray, G.A. et al. (2004). Consumption of high-fructose corn syrup in beverages may play a role in the epidemic of obesity. *American Journal of Clinical Nutrition*, vol. 79, pp. 537-543.

Bray, G.A. (2010). Soft drink consumption and obesity: it is all about fructose. *Current Opinion in Lipidology*, vol. 21, pp. 51-57.

Brazilian Institute of Geography and Statistiocial Communication. (2011). Brazil: IBGE.

Centers for Disease Control (2004). Trends in intake of energy and macronutrients – United States, 1971-2000. *Morbidity and Mortality Weekly Report*, vol. 53, pp. 80-82.

Brazilian Institute of Geography and Statistics. (2009). Nutritional status and household food availability in Brazil. Brazil: IBGE.

Brazilian Institute of Geography and Statistics. (2011). Analysis of individual food consumption in Brazil. Brazil: IBGE.

Bueno, M.B., Marchioni, D.M.L., Cesar, C.L.G., Fisberg, R.M. (2012). Added sugar: Consumption and associated factors among adults and the elderly. *Revista Brasileira de Epidemiologia*, vol. 15, pp. 256-264.

Buyse, J., & Geuns, J.M.C. (2004) *The safety of stevioside*. Heverlee: Euprint ed.

Chanmugam, P., Guthrie, J.F., Cecilio, S., Morton, J.F., Basiotis, P.P., & Anand, R. (2003). Did fat intake in the United States really decline between 1989-1991 and 1994-1996? *Journal of the American Dietetic Association*, vol. 103, pp. 867-872.

Chen, J., Jeppesen, P.B., Abudula, R., Dyrskog, S.E.U., Clombo, M., & Hermansen, K. (2006). Stevioside does not cause increased basal insulin secretion or beta-cell desensitization as does the sulphonylurea, glibenclamide: Studies in vitro. *Life Science*, vol. 78, pp. 1748-1753.

Chen, J., Jeppesen, P.B., Nordentoft, I, Hermansen, K. (2007). Stevioside improves pancreatic beta-cell function during glucotoxicity via regulation of acetyl-CoA carboxylase. *American Journal of Physiology – Endocrinology and Metabolism*, vol. 292, pp. 1906-1916.

Chen, X., Hermansen, K., Xiao, J., Bystrup, S.K., O'Driscoll, L., & Jeppesen, P.B. (2012). Isosteviol has beneficial effects on palmitate-induced α-cell dysfunction and gene expression. *PLoS One*, 7(3), pp. 34361

Choi, Y.K., Johlin, Jr. F.C., Summers, R.W., Jackson, M., Rao, & S.S. (2003). Fructose intolerance: an under-recognized problem. *American Journal of Gastroenterology*, vol. 98, pp. 1348-1353.

Chong, M.F., Fielding, B.A., & Frayn, K.N. (2007). Mechanisms for the acute effect of fructose on postprandial lipemia. *American Journal of Clinical Nutrition*, vol. 85, pp. 1511-1520.

Cohen, A.M. et al. (1966). Effect of interchanging bread and sucrose as main source of carbohydrate in low fat diet on the glucose tolerance curve of healthy volunteer subjects. *American Journal of Clinical Nutrition*, vol. 19, pp. 59-62.

Deer N. (1949-50). *The history of sugar*. London, UK: Chapman and Hall.

Dentin, R., Benhamed, F., Hainault, I., Fauveau, V., Foufelle, F., Dyck, J.R.B., Birard, J., & Postic, C. (2006). Liver-specific inhibition of ChREBP improves hepatic steatosis and insulin resistance in ob/ob mice. *Diabetes*, vol. 55, pp. 2159-2170.

Dyrskog, S.E.U., Jeppesen, P.B., Colombo, M., Abudula, R., & Hermansen, K. (2005). Preventive effects of a soy-based diet supplemented with stevioside on development of the metabolic syndrome and type 2 diabetes in Zucker diabetic fatty rats. *Metabolism*, vol. 54, pp. 1181-1188.

Edwards, D.M. et al. (1999). Glucagon-like peptide 1 has a physiological role in the control of postprandial glucose in humans: studies with the antagonist exendin 9.39. *Diabetes*, vol. 48, pp. 86-93.

Elliott, S.S. et al. (2002). Fructose, weight gain, and the insulin resistance syndrome. *American Journal of Clinical Nutrition*, vol. 76, pp. 911-922.

Fung, T.T., Malik, V., Rexrode, K.M., Willett, W.C., & Hu, F.B. (2009). Sweetened beverage consumption and risk of coronary heart disease in women. *American Journal of Clinical Nutrition*, vol. 89, pp. 1037-1042.

Galloway, J.H. (1989). *The sugar cane industry*. Cambridge: Cambridge University Press.

Gao, X.B., Qi, L., Qiao, N., Choi, H.K., Curhan, G., Tucker, K.L., & Ascherio, A. (2007). Intake of added sugar and sugar-sweetended drink and serum uric acid concentration in US men and women. *Hypertension*, vol. 50, pp. 306-312.

Grupo de investigacion de la Red Qualidiab. (2001). Evaluación de la calidad de atencion al paciente con diabetes en Latino America. *Pan American Journal of public Health*, vol. 10, pp. 309-317.

Hallfrisch, J. (1990). Metabolic effects of dietary fructose. *FASEB Journal*, vol. 4, pp. 2652-2660.

Havel, P.J. (2002). Control of energy homeostasis and insulin action by adipocyte hormones: leptin, acylation stimulating protein, and adiponectin. *Current Opinion in Lipidology*, vol. 13, pp. 51-59.

Helmchen, L.A., & Henderson, R.M. (2004). Changes in the distribution of body mass index of white US men, 1890-2000. *Annals of Human Biology*, vol. 31, pp. 174-182.

Hong, J., Abudula, R., Chen, J., Jeppesen, P.B., Rolfsen, S.E.D. Xiao, J., Colombo, M., & Hermansen, K. (2005). The short-term effect of fatty acids on glucagon secretion is influenced by their chain length, spatial configuration, and degree of unsaturation. Studies in vitro. *Metabolism*, vol. 54, issue 10, pp. 1329-1336.

Hong, J., Chen, L., Jeppesen, P.B., Nordentoft, I., & Hermansen, K. (2006). Stevioside counteracts the alpha cell hypersecretion caused by long-term palmitate exposure. *American Journal of Physiology – Endocrinology and Metabolism*, vol. 290, pp. 416-422.

Hudgins, L.C., Hellerstein, M., Seidman, C., Neese, R., Diakun, J., & Hirsch, J. (1996). Human fatty acid synthesis is stimulated by a eucaloric low fat, high carbohydrate diet. *Journal of Clinical Investigation*, vol. 97, pp. 2081-2091.

Hudgins, L.C., Seidman, C.E., Diakun, J., & Hirsch, J. (1998). Human fatty acid synthesis is reduced after the substitution of dietary starch for sugar. *American Journal of Clinical Nutrition*, vol. 67, pp. 631-639.

Hudgins, L.C., Hellerstein, M.K., Seidman, C.E., Neese, R.A., Tremaroli, J.D., & Hirsch, J. (2000). Relationship between carbohydrate-induced hypertriglyceridemia and fatty acid synthesis in lean and obese subjects. *Journal of Lipid Research*, vol. 41, pp. 595-604.

Hudgins, L.C., Parker, T.S., Levine, D.M., & Hellerstein, M.K. (2011). A dual sugar challenge test for lipogenic sensitivity to dietary fructose. *Journal of Clinical Endocrinology and Metabolism*, vol. 96, pp. 861-868.

Israel, K.D. et al. (1998). Serum uric acid, inorganic phosphorus, and glutamic-oxalacetic transaminase and blood pressure in carbohydrate-sensitive adults consuming three different levels of sucrose. *Annals of Nutrition and Metabolism*, vol. 27, pp. 425-435.

James, J. et al. (2004). Preventing childhood obesity by reducing consumption of carbonated drinks: cluster randomized comtrolled trial. *BMJ*, vol. 328, pp. 1237-1241.

Jeppesen, P.B. et al. (2000). Stevioside acts directly on the pancreatic beta-cell to secrete insulin: Actions independent of cAMP and ATP-sensitive K-channel activity. *Metabolism*, vol. 49, pp. 2008-2214.

Jeppesen, P.B., Gregersen, S., Alstrup, K. K., & Hermansen, K. (2002). Stevioside induces anti-hyperglycaemic, insulinotropic and glucagonostatic effects in vivo: Studies in the diabetic Goto-Kakizaki (GK) rats. *Phytomedicine*, vol. 9, pp. 9-14.

Jeppesen, P.B., Gregersen, S., Rolfsen, S.E.D., Jepsen, M., Colombo, M., Agger, A., Xiao, J., Kruhøffer, M., Ørntoft, T., & Hermansen, K. (2003). Anti-hyperglycemic and blood pressure-reducing effects of stevioside in the diabetic Goto-Kakizaki (GK) rat. *Metabolism*, vol. 52, pp. 372-378.

Jeppesen, P.B., Rolfsen, S.E.D., Agger, A., Gregersen, S., Colombo, M., Xiao, J., & Hermansen, K. (2006). Can stevioside in combination with a soy-based dietary supplement be a new useful treatment of type 2 diabetes? An in vivo study in the diabetic goto-kakizaki rat. *Review of Diabetic Studies*, vol. 3, pp. 189-199.

Johnson, R.J., Segal, M.S., Sautin, Y., Nakagawa, T., Feig, D.I., Kang, D.H., Gersch, M.S., Benner, S., & Sánchez-Lozada, L.G. (2006a). Potential role of sugar (fructose) in the epidemic of hypertension, obesity and the metabolic syndrome, diabetes, kidney disease, and cardiovascular disease. *American Journal of Clinical Nutrition*, vol. 86, pp. 899-906.

Johnson, R.K, Appel, L.J., Brands, M., Howard, B.V., Lefevre, M., Lustig, R.H., Sacks, F., Steffen, L., & Wylie-Rosett, J., on behalf of the American Heart Association Nutrition Committee of the Council on Nutrition Physical Activity and Metabolism, and the Council on Epidemiology and Prevention. (2009). Dietary sugar intake and cardiovascular health. A scientific statement from the American Heart Association. *Circulation*, vol. 120, pp. 1011-1120.

Jurgens, H. et al. (2005). Consuming fructose-sweetened beverages increases body adiposity in mice. *Obesity Research*, vol. 13, pp. 1146-1156.

Kneepkens, C.M., Vonk, R.J., & Fernandes, J. (1984). Incomplete intestinal absorption of fructose. *Archives of Disease in Childhood*, vol. 59, pp. 735-738.

Koo, W.W., & Taylor, R.D. (2013). 2012 outlook of the U.S. and world sugar markets, 2011-2012. Agribusiness & Applied Econimics Report 692, North Dakota State University. Retrieved from http://agecon.lib.umn.edu/

Ludwig, D.S. et al. (2001). Relation between consumption of sugar-sweetened drinks and childhood obesity: a prospective, observational analysis. *Lancet*, vol. 357, pp. 505-508.

Lustig, R.H. (2010). Fructose: Metabolic, Hedonic, and Societal Parallels with ethanol. *Journal ofthe American Dietetic Association*, vol. 110, pp. 1307-1321.

Lustig, R.H, Schmidt, L.A., & Brindis, C.D. (2012). Public health: The toxic truth about sugar. *Nature*, vol. 482, pp. 27-29

Maersk, M., Belza, A., Stødkilde-Jørgensen, H., Ringgaard, S., Chabanova, E., Thomsen, H., Pedersen, S.B., Astrup, A., & Richelsen, B. (2012). Sucrose-sweetened beverages increase fat storage in the liver, muscle, and visceral fat depot: a 6-mo randomized intervention study. *American Journal of Cinical Nutrition*, vol. 95, pp. 283-289.

Ministry of Health. (2006). Dietary Guidelines for the Brazilian Population. Brazil: Ministry of Health.

Nature. (2012). vol. 482, pp. 27-29. doi: 10.1038/482027a2

Nagai, Y., Yonemitsu, S., Erion, D.M., Iwasaki, T., Stark, R., Weismann, D., Dong, J., Zhang, D., Jurezak, M.J., Loffler, M.G., Cresswell, J., Yu, X.X., Murray, S.F., Bhanot, S., Monia, B.P., Bogan, J.S., Samuel, V., & Shulman, G.I. (2009). The role of peroxisome proliferator-activated receptor gamma coactivator-1 beta in the pathogenesis of fructose-induced insulin resistance. *Cell Metabolism*, vol. 9, pp. 252-264.

Nakagawa, T., Tuttle, K.R., Short, R., Johnson, & R.J. (2005). Hypothesis: fructose-induced hyperuricemia as a causal mechanism for the epidemic of the metabolic syndrome. *Nature Clinicak Practice Nephrology*, vol. 1, pp. 80-86.

Nakagawa, T. et al. (2006b). A causal role for uric acid in fructose-induced metabolic syndrome. *American Journal of Physiology – Renal Physiology*, 290, pp. 625-631.

Nordentoft, I., Jeppesen, P.B., Hong, J., Abudula, R., & Hermansen, K. (2008). Isosteviol increases insulin sensitivity and changes gene expression of key insulin regulatory genes and transcription factors in islets of the diabetic KKAy-mouse. *Diabetes, Obesity and Metabolism*, vol. 10, pp. 939-949.

Nguyen, S., Choi, H.K., Lustig, R.H., & Hsu, C.Y. (2009). Sugar sweetened beverages, serum uric acid, and blood pressure in adolescents. *Journal of Pediatrics*, vol. 154, pp. 807-813.

Nishida, C., Uauy, R., Kumanyika, S., & Shetty, P. (2004). The Joint WHO/FAO Expert Consultation on diet, nutrition and the prevention of chronic diseases: process, product and policy implications. *Public Health Nutrition*, vol. 7, pp. 245-250.

Parks, E.J., & Hellerstein, M.K. (2000). Carbohydrate-induced hypertriacylglycerolemia: historical perspective and review of biological mechanisms. *American Journal of Clinical Nutrition*, vol. 71, pp. 412-433.

Parks, E.J., Skokan, L.E., Timlin, M.T., & Dingfelder, C.S. (2008). Dietary sugars stimulate fatty acid synthesis in adults. *Journal of Nutrition*, vol. 138, pp. 1039-1046.

Petersen, K.F. et al. (2001). Stimulating thesis in humans. *Diabetes*, vol. 50, pp. 1263-1268.

Petersen, K.F., Dufour, S., Savage, D.B., Bilz, S., Solomon, G., Yonemitsu, S., Cline, G.W., Befroy, D., Zemany, L., Kahn, B.B., Papademetris, X., Rothman, D.L., & Shulman, G.I. (2007). The role of skeletal muscle insulin resistance in the pathogenesis of the metabolic syndrome. *PNAS USA*, vol. 104, pp. 12587-12594.

Raben, A. et al. (2002). Sucrose compared with artificial sweeteners: different effects on ad libitum food intake and body weight after 10 wk of supplementation in overweight subjects. *American Journal of Clinical Nutrition*, vol. 76, pp. 721-729.

Rasmussen, J.J., & Gudmand-Høyer, E. (1986). Absorption capacity of fructose in healthy adults. Comparison with sucrose and its constituent monosaccharides. *Gut*, vol. 27, pp. 1161-1168.

Ravich, W.J., Bayless, T.M., & Thomas, M. (1983). Fructose: incomplete intestinal absorption in humans. *Gastroenterology*, vol. 84, pp. 26-29.

Reziwanggu, A., Jeppesen, P.B., Rolfsen, S.E.D., Xiao, J., & Hermansen, K. (2004). Rebaudioside A potently stimulates insulin secretion from isolated mouse islets: Studies on the dose-, glucose- and calcium-dependency. *Metabolism*, vol. 53, pp. 1378-1381.

Saad, M.F. et al. (1998). Physiological insulinemia acutely modulated plasma leptin. *Diabetes*, vol. 47, pp. 544-549.

Sharman, M.J. et al. (2004). Very low-carbohydrate and low-fat diets affect fasting lipids and postprandial lipemia differently in overweight men. *Journal of Nutrition*, vol. 134, pp. 880-855.

Sheridan, R.B. (1973). *Sugar and slavery*. Baltimore: Johns Hopkins University Press.

Schwarz, J.M. et al. (1989). Thermogenesis in men and women induced by fructose vs glucose added to a meal. *American Journal of Clinical Nutrition*, vol. 49, pp. 667-674.

Stanhope, K.L., & Havel, P.J. (2008). Fructose consumption: potential mechanisms for its effects to increase visceral adiposity and induce dyslipidemia and insulin resistance. *Current Opinion in Lipidology*, vol. 19, pp. 16-24.

Taylor, E.N., & Curhan, G.C. (2008). Fructose consumption and the risk of kidney stones. *Kidney International*, vol. 73, pp. 489-496.

Truswell, A.S., Seach, J.M., & Thorburn, A.W. (1988). Incomplete absorption of pure fructose in healthy subjects and the facilitating effect of glucose. *American Journal of Clinical Nutrition*, vol. 48, pp. 1424-1430.

US Census Bureau. (2003). Statistical abstract of the US. no 214, 2003.

Verna, E.C., & Berk, P.D. (2008). Role of fatty acids in the pathogenesis of obesity and fatty liver: Impact of bariatric surgery. *Seminars in Liver Disease*, vol. 28, pp. 407-226.

Vos, M.B., Kimmons, J.E., Gillespic, C., Welsh, J., & Blanck, H.M. (2008). Dietary fructose consumption among US children and adults: The third National Health and Nutrition Examination Survey. *Medscape Journal of Medicine*, vol. 10, p 160.

World Health Statistics. Obesity data used is from 2008 – latest updated 2011. Retrieved from: www.who.int/gho

Yudkin J. (1972). Sugar and disease. *Nature*, vol. 239, pp. 197-199.

Zivkovic, A.M., German, J.B., & Sanyal, A.J. (2007). Comparative review of diets for the metabolic syndrome: Implication for nonalcoholic fatty liver disease. *American Journal of Clinical Nutrition*, vol. 86, pp. 285-300.

PART TWO:
THE PREFERENCE
FOR SWEETNESS

Opening Remarks

By Susanne Højlund

Why do we like sweetness? The human preference for this certain taste is often explained as a natural, physiological fact related to the newborn baby and its need for breast feeding. Human breast milk is sweet, and the idea is that we learn to prefer this taste from the very beginning, retaining the inherent preference for the rest of our lives. But there is more to be said on the subject than this, we believe. As Sidney Mintz has shown in his many analyses of the role of sugar in modernity, the taste of sweetness is not only introduced to us through the infant-mother relationship; it is also regulated macro-sociologically by many other factors. Taste is thus a broad concept that covers many meanings, from the taste buds on one's tongue to lifestyle and identity. To taste something or to express a certain taste preference is a complex process mediated between substance, body, mind, and culture/society. It implies multiple processes, including physiologically recognizing a certain quality of food; categorizing it as a taste; judging whether it is something you like or not; relating this assessment to former knowledge, memories, traditions, health discourses, and morality; adjusting your actual tasting practice to the social context; and so on. As such, taste is both natural and cultural. In order to understand the meaning of sweetness we must therefore adopt an interdisciplinary approach.

In this part of the book, we explore the human preference for sweetness through two different but complementary approaches to taste. The first understands taste as a relation between the substance 'sugar' (mostly sucrose) and the ability of the human taste buds to recognize this substance under certain conditions. Ulla Kidmose and Heidi Kildegaard analyze how "the gustatory sense" can be measured and perceived, before investigating the relation between obesity and sweetness preference. Through this in-depth literature review they provide an illuminating insight into contemporary scientific knowledge about the ability to taste and differentiate sweetness. They conclude that there is no one-to-one relationship between taste buds, perception, and lifestyle diseases such as obesity, and they point to the need for supplementing studies of cultural factors that have an impact on tasting ability and taste preferences.

The second chapter follows up on this perceived gap in our knowledge with its cultural approach to taste, illustrated with an analysis of the role of sugar in Cuba. Few populations in the world have experienced such rapid and dramatic changes directly related to sugar as that of Cuba. At a time when the so-called lifestyle diseases are on the increase, and sugar is the suspected cause, Cuba is an interesting place to study the relationship between lifestyle and sugar consumption. In this article, it is argued that the study of how sugar finds its way into the Cuban body goes through an analysis of taste as a cultural sense. The roles played by eating sweet food and drinking sweet drinks in daily life are not simply a matter of an individual preference for sweetness; they are also bound up with societal conditions and cultural values. Højlund discusses what sugar and sweetness mean to being Cuban, arguing that the taste of sweetness carries memories of times gone by. Through this she shows how the taste of sweetness is an integrated part of both personal identity and contemporary cultural patterns. The taste of sweetness in a Cuban context, though, is more than a sweet memory: it also reminds the Cubans of hard times, when sugar was the only way to satisfy your appetite. Paradoxically, during this period both diabetes and coronary disease were less prevalent. Throughout these examples the chapter stresses that the Cuban preference for sweetness is one story, and that other places will reveal other stories behind the human "sweet tooth."

CHAPTER II

Sweetness Preference, Sugar Intake, and Obesity in Latin America

By Ulla Kidmose and Heidi Kildegaard

Taste is a very important determinant for food intake: if you like the taste of the food you will eat it! The sweet taste of sugar often contributes to high liking and food preferences. Children are born with a high sweetness preference due to the sweet taste of breast milk, but there are many other factors besides this preference that may affect sugar intake and the onset of obesity. The relationship between sweetness perception, high liking and preference of sweet food and sugar intake as well as obesity is elucidated in this chapter.

The sensory quality of food is evaluated by humans using their five senses: i) the *gustatory sense* (the sense of taste), which is situated on the surface of the tongue and the palate in the mouth; ii) the *olfactory sense* (the sense of smell) in the nose; iii) the *sense of vision* in the eye; iv) the *sense of hearing* in the ear; and v) the *sense of touch* on the surface of skin. The sense of taste is a chemical sense, since chemical compounds are registered by the taste buds on the tongue and the soft palate in the mouth. On the tongue four classical basic tastes are detected: sweetness, bitterness, sourness, and saltiness. Additionally, umami is counted as the fifth taste (Lawless & Heymann 1998). Taste buds are clustered in groups of 30-50 cells, forming balls or onion-shaped structures. Pores on the top of the taste buds connect them to the fluid environment of the saliva in the mouth. Following the ingestion of food, taste molecules are dissolved in the saliva and the pores situated on the taste buds detect these molecules. From the taste buds, gustatory signals are transmitted to peripheral nerves which transmit taste sensation signals to the brain (Meilgaard et al. 2007). During this process, a specific taste quality perception is generated allowing sugars to be differentiated from other compounds in foods. Hence, the term 'sensory perception' designates the act of becoming aware of a stimulus and its qualities.

Sensory perceptions are created by both the sensations that are triggered and the brain's interpretation of these sensations. The interpretation of sensations is often based on previous experience. Hence, sensory perception involves chemical and physiological reactions in combination with human psychology and it varies between individuals.

Perception of taste intensity allows the taste buds to detect different concentrations of sweet tasting compounds, but due to individual differences in taste perception, it is not possible for anyone to determine the absolute concentration of a sweet tasting compound (Lawless & Haymann 2010; McCaughey 2008; Meilgaard et al. 2007). The lowest concentration of a substance such as sucrose or the minimum intensity required for detection of a sweet stimulus is defined as the *absolute threshold value* for sweetness. Threshold values of sweetness vary between individuals due to factors such as age, gender, and illness and are strongly associated with how sweet a product is expected to be. Meilgaard et al. (2007) examined the threshold values for sucrose in 47 individuals and found that the range of the threshold values for sucrose varied between 0.08g/100mL and 2.56g/100mL.

Many studies have shown that children have lower taste sensitivity than adults (Glanville, Kaplan, & Fischer 1964; James, Laing, & Oram 1997; Mela 2001), though a few studies have reported that children aged 5-7 and 8-9 years have detection threshold values similar to that of adults (Anliker et al. 1991; James et al. 2004). This lower sensitivity means that children simply require higher levels of e.g. sweetness in foods to achieve the same perception of sweetness intensity experienced by adults. Zandstra and de Graff (1998) showed that with increasing sucrose concentration the perception of sweetness increased by a lower gradient in children aged 6-12 years compared to older children and adults. It is also known that as people get older the threshold of stimuli needed to excite taste sensations increases (Meilgaard, Civille, & Carr 2007; Mojet, Christ-Hazelhof, & Heidema 2001). In a study by Mojet, Christ-Hazelhof, and Heidema (2001), the detection thresholds for several tastants were determined for 21 young and older men and women, respectively. They found an overall effect for age as well as a gender-age interaction for detection thresholds of sucrose: older men were less sensitive to sweetness than young people, and tended to be less sensitive than older women. These results indicate that changes occur in taste sensitivity and hence sweetness perception across life span.

SWEET TASTE AND SWEET COMPOUNDS

To be perceived as sweet after ingestion, food molecules need to fit into specific receptors situated on the taste buds on the tongue. Simple sugars, which are perceived as sweet, include sucrose, fructose, glucose, galactose, lactose, and maltose. In both sugar beet root and sugar cane, sweetness is due to the presence of a high content of sucrose as described in detail in "Production methods and quality of sugar cane in Latin America" (Bjoern & Kidmose 2013). Other compounds that also have a sweet taste include inulin, which is present in high quantities in Jerusalem artichokes, many alcohols like xylitol and sorbitol glycerol, and steviosides, which originate from the leaves of the South American plant *Stevia rebaudiana*. In recent years, new sweeteners such as aspartame and acesulfam K have been manufactured; many of these synthetic sweeteners have a very high intensity of sweetness compared to sucrose (Cardello et al. 1999; Cardoso & Bolini 2007).

Assessment of the relative sweetness of different sugars or sweet compounds is rather difficult since the perception of sweetness is individual. In general, methods used to determine relative sweetness intensity include paired comparisons, the constant stimulus method, and magnitude estimation (Cardello, Da Silva, & Damasio 1999). Using these methods, potency (defined as the number of times sweeter a compound is than an iso-sweet concentration of sucrose) can be assessed. The sweetness potency of stevioside and aspartame are 160 and 100-200, respectively, whereas the potency of glucose and fructose are slightly lower and higher than sucrose, respectively. Sweetness potency depends on the concentration of sucrose, pH, and temperature.

SWEETNESS, PREFERENCE, AND LIKING

Sensory analysis encompasses both objective and subjective sensory evaluations. The subjective sensory evaluation includes consumer tests. These are affective tests, a general class of sensory tests that assess the acceptability or degree of liking of a set of food products. When discussing subjective sensory evaluation by consumers, we use two key terms: *Liking and preference.* Consumers' liking and preferences are measured or assessed using two different methods. Liking or acceptance of food can be evaluated using a rating test. In hedonic rating tests, products are evaluated on a line scale or an interval scale and the food is evaluated according to how much it is liked. Hedonic scales may be 9-point, 7-point, or 5-point scales. They allow the participant to express positive, indifferent, or negative reactions, as shown in Figure 1.

Like it
very much

Do not like
it at all

Figure 1. A smiley 7-point hedonic scale (Kildegaard 2011).

The term *preference* is also used in relation to consumer tests and refers to an individual's preference for one product over another. In general, preference tests do not use hedonic scales but rather ranking tests. In a ranking test, two or more products are compared according to preference. Individuals are asked to rank products in either descending or ascending order of preference, as shown in Figure 2 (Kildegaard 2011). However, these tests are not very informative about the magnitude of liking or disliking of the product since preference does not necessarily reflect liking. One product may be preferred over another without being liked at all (Lawless & Heymann 2010). In consumer science and physiology, the term preference is often used instead of liking.

Most liked

Least liked

Figure 2. An example of a ranking test. The consumers were served 5 food products, each with a 3-digit code and after tasting the samples they were asked to rank the products from most to least liked by writing the 3-digit codes in the boxes (Kildegaard 2011).

In general, both food preference and liking are very subjective terms and depend very much on the individual. Personal factors form a significant part of taste perception, as described in the section "The sweet taste, sensitivity, and perception." The individual's unique perception of a food will have an influence how much they like it. Earlier it was assumed that sweetness percep-

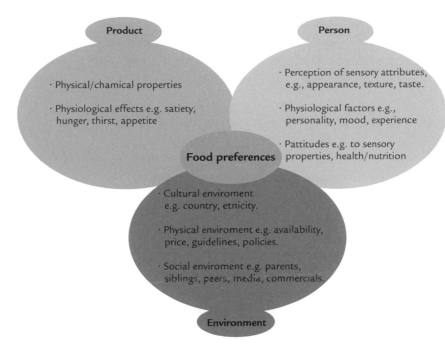

Figure 3. *Overview of factors influencing children's food preferences and food choices (Kildegaard 2011; adapted from Shepherd & Pro-children framework 1989).*

tion predicted sweet preferences. However, this assumption is not necessarily true (Drewnowski 1997). Besides personal factors, food preference and liking are also influenced by various food-related and environmental factors. These factors are elucidated in Figure 3.

Liking is one of the major determinants for food intake, food choice, and eating habits. Several studies have shown that children's liking is highly predictive of their intake (Birch 1979; Birch & Sullivan 1991; Gibson, Wardle, & Watts 1998). Moreover, cultural, sociological, social, and individual factors, such as physiological factors, age, gender, and attitudes, affect our food preferences, liking, and eating behaviour (Fig. 3) (Kildegaard 2011; Birch 1999; Reed et al. 1997; Drewnowski 1997; Nicklaus et al. 2004).

The development of human preferences and liking is a result of the interaction between genetic predispositions and environmental and learned factors (Birch 1999). Infants have an innate preference for sweet tastes and they prefer sugar solutions to water and sweeter solutions to less sweet solutions, in contrast to adults (De Graaf & Zandstra 1999; Desor, Maller, & Turner 1973; Nisbett & Gurwitz 1970). The innate preference for sweet tastes can be ascribed to the fact that infants are adapted to the sweet taste of breast milk immediately after birth. Moreover, sweet foods are in general safe foods, in contrast to bitter tasting foods; bitterness is often a result of a high content of toxic compounds (Holt et al. 2000).

CHANGING THE PREFERENCE AND LIKING FOR SWEETNESS

Studies have shown a decline in sweetness preference as children become adults that may be caused by a shift in taste sensitivity of sweetness (Desor & Beauchamp 1987; Nicklaus et al. 2004). It is observed that children live in a different chemical sensory world from adults, as evidenced by their higher preference for sweet and sour tasting foods (Darwin 1877). In addition, preference for and liking of sweet tastes can be modified through repeated exposures to these tastes (Liem & Graaf 2004; Beauchamp & Moran 1984; Holt et al. 2000). A study in which infants were repeatedly exposed to sweetened water showed that at two years of age these infants had a high preference for sweeter-tasting water (Beauchamp & Moran 1984). Liem and de Graff (2004) showed that when both children and adults experienced repeated exposure to sweet orangeades with added sucrose, only the children developed a significantly increased preference for sweet orangeade after the exposure period. These children also tended to consume more orangeade during the last day compared to the first day of intervention.

In contrast, the preference for sweet orangeade did not change in the adult participants; they consumed significantly less during the last day compared to the first day of intervention (Liem & de Graaf 2004). In a study by Sartor et al. (2011), normal-weight adult subjects were divided into sucrose-likers and sucrose-dislikers before a four-week soft drink supplementation period ($\approx$760ml soft drink/day). Only the sucrose-dislikers significantly increased their preference towards sweetness after the soft drink supplementation period; the sucrose-likers did not experience any change.

In summary, alteration of sweetness preference after repeated exposure to sweet food can occur, but several factors such as age and initial sweetness preference influence the effects of repeated exposure.

PREFERENCE AND LIKING FOR SWEET TASTES AND SUGAR INTAKE

As described in the previous section, many children have a high preference for sweet tastes. Several studies have shown that a high preference for sweet tastes has a strong correlation with a high consumption of sugary foods (Cooke & Wardle 2005; Pangborn & Giovanni 1984; Holt et al. 2000). Many sugary foods are associated with a high energy density, and consumption of high energy-dense foods may contribute to disruption of the body's energy balance, causing obesity. Duffy et al. (2003) explored whether markers of taste variation were associated with variability in sweetness sensation, sweetness preference, and intake of added sugar. They used 6-n-propylthiouracil (PROP) and quinine hydrochloride (QHCL) to predict sweetness in solutions and foods since perceived bitterness of PROP and quinine has been shown to correlate with sweetness preference. By using multiple regression analyses they found that both PROP and QHCL contributed independently to the prediction of sweetness sensation, preference, and intake with effects that were separated from those of sex and adiposity. Individuals who tasted PROP as least bitter and QHCL as most bitter reported the greatest preference for and intake of added sugars. On the basis of these results it is concluded that measures of taste variation showed significant correlation with sweetness sensation and preference, as well as sugar intake. In addition, these results also showed that elevated sweetness preferences are associated with a high intake of added sugars and consumption of sweet food, and vice versa. These findings were in accordance with Holt et al. 2000. In contrast, other studies have failed to show this relationship (Mattes & Mela 1986). According to Drewnowski (1997), the lack of relationship between sweetness preferences and sugar intake might be caused by the fact that individuals restrict their intake of sweet foods due to their knowledge of weight-related and nutritional factors.

THE RELATION BETWEEN PREFERENCE FOR SWEET TASTES, SUGAR INTAKE, AND OBESITY

The rates of obesity in Latin America have been increasing as the region's countries emerge from poverty. Estimation of the prevalence of obesity in the Latin American population varies from 9.9% to 35.7% (Filozof et al. 2001; Bautista et al. 2009). Urban populations and women are the most affected groups (Bautista et al. 2009). In five Latin American countries between 1994 and 1996, the prevalence of obesity in women varied between 1.4-7.6%, while the prevalence of childhood obesity varied between 2.1-12.1%. The prevalence of obesity in Latin America seems to be independent of socioeconomic status and educational level (Uauy, Albala, & Kain 2001). The crucial factors contributing to the rise in obesity seem to be dietary changes and increased inactivity. Dietary changes include an increased intake of energy-dense food rich in fat and carbohydrates (Bautista et al. 2009; Uauy, Albala, & Kain 2001).

A relevant question in the search for solutions to this epidemic has to be whether sweetness perception and preference for and liking of sweet food can be directly linked to the increased prevalence of obesity in Latin America, since these parameters may be associated with obesity? This relationship has been called the "sweet tooth theory" (Snyder et al. 2006; Drewnowski 1997). The hypothesis was that heightened preference for and intake of sweet foods was directly correlated to obesity (Rodin, Moskowitz, & Bray 1978; Drewnowski 1997). In Latin America, sugar is very readily available since many of its countries produce large quantities of sugar cane (Bjørn & Kidmose 2011).

Few studies have investigated how preferences for sweetness are related to food intake and obesity. Although the evidence is scarce, preferences do seem to relate to obesity – but not necessarily preferences for sweetness. Snyder et al. (2006) showed that liking of sweet foods increased with BMI for the same perceived sweetness. Matsushita et al. (2009) also found a positive association between a preference for sweet tastes and weight increase among women. A study by Sharma and Hedge (2009) compared the food preferences of normal-weight and obese pre-teen children (n=500). They found that 51.1% of overweight and obese children preferred sweet and fatty foods frequently, compared to 24.2% of the normal-weight and under-weight children. Concordantly, 53% of the underweight and normal-weight children preferred not sweet and fatty foods compared to 18.2% of the overweight and obese children.

These results suggest that children who already need to pay attention to their weight like and consume more sweet and fatty foods (which are typically energy-dense and highly palatable) than their leaner counterparts (Sharma & Hedge 2009). Davis et al. (2011) found that preferences for sweet and fatty foods were positively correlated with various eating variables that accounted for the variance in BMI. Sator et al. (2011) investigated differences in sweet taste perception and implicit attitude toward sweetness using an implicit association test (IAT) between normal-weight and overweight/obese adults. The study showed that the obese adults perceived sweet tastes as less intense (-23%) and reported 2.1 times higher IAT scores for sweetness than normal-weight controls. It was concluded that obese individuals were more implicitly attracted to sweetness than normal-weight individuals. These findings indicate that there are some differences in food preferences between normal-weight and obese subjects, particularly with regards to sweet and fatty foods.

In contrast to the studies that showed a positive relationship between high preference for and consumption of sweet food and obesity, other studies using sucrose solutions, sweetened soft drinks, or chocolate milkshakes found no correlation between sweetness preferences and body weight (Drewnowski 1997). Cox et al. (1999) showed in a human intervention study with obese and lean consumers that there was no difference in liking of foods with different taste qualities between the two groups. Instead, they found that foods classified as "salty/savoury" foods contributed with significantly more energy compared to food classified as "sweet" and that obese subjects derived more energy from foods classified as "salty/savoury", which were correlated with a diet higher in energy density than the lean subjects.

These results were supported by Drewnowski et al. (1985), who found that obese subjects preferred high-fat stimuli (>34% lipid) that contained less than 5% sucrose, in contrast to normal-weight subjects that optimally preferred stimuli containing 20% lipid and less than 10% sucrose. In a review of Mela (1996), it was concluded that consumption of diets moderate or high in fat or energy density combined with low physical activity as well as several other factors (e.g. genetic predisposition, cognitive restraints) appear to be critical contributors to development of obesity. Furthermore, Mela (1996) also claimed that preferences for and consumption of dietary fat are linked to weight status based on existing literature.

With respect to differences in preference for sweet and fatty food, ethnicity also seems to play a part. In a study of the food preferences of whites and Pima Indians, the Pima Indians rated solutions that vary in sugar and fat content significantly sweeter than whites, and women also rated sweetness higher than men. The Pima Indians liked sweet and creamy solutions less than the white participants did. Moreover, a heightened hedonic response to these solutions among the Pima Indians was associated with weight gain (Salbe et al. 2004).

In summary, it is difficult to conclude whether sweetness perception, liking, and preferences influence sugar intake as well as development of obesity or result in differences in obese subjects compared to lean subjects; the matter remains unresolved. Inconsistent results reported in different studies over many decades combined with the different designs and set-ups of these studies prevent us making any clear and unambiguous conclusions. Sugar intake and obesity are very complex issues, and both are affected by multiple factors, as has been shown in this review.

BIBLIOGRAPHY

Anliker, J.A., Bartoshuk, L., Ferris, A.M., & Hooks, L.D. (1991). Children's food preferences and genetic sensitivity to the bitter taste of 6-Normal-Propylthiouracil (Prop). *American Journal of Clinical Nutrition*, vol. 54, issue 2, pp. 316-320.

Bautista, L.E., Casas, J.P., Herrera, V.M., Miranda, J.J., Perel, P., Pichardo, R., González, A., Sanchez, J. R., Ferreccio, C., Aguilera, X., Silva, E., Oróstegui, M., Gómez, L.F., Chirinos, J. A., Medina-Lezama, J., Pérez, C.M., Suárez, E., Oritz, A.P., Rosero, L., Schapochnik, N., Ortiz, Z., & Ferrante, D. (2009). The Latin American Consortium of Studies in Obesity (LASO). *Obesity Reviews*, vol. 10, pp. 364-370.

Beauchamp, G.K., & Moran, M. (1984). Acceptance of sweet and salty tastes in 2-year-old children. *Appetite*, vol. 5 issue 4, pp. 291-305.

Birch, L.L. (1979). Dimensions of preschool children's food preferences. *Journal of Nutrition Education*, vol. 11, issue 2, pp. 77-80.

Birch, L.L. (1999). Development of food preferences. *Annual Review of Nutrition,* vol. 19, pp. 41-62.

Birch, L.L., & Sullivan, S.A. (1991). Measuring children's food freferences. *Journal of School Health*, vol. 61, issue 5, pp. 212-214.

Bjørn, G.K., & Kidmose, U. (2013). Production methods and quality of sugar cane in Latin America. In this volume (pp. 117-125).

Cardello, H.M.A.B., Da Silva, M.A.P.A., & Damasio, M.H. (1999). Measurement of the relative sweetness of stevia extract, aspartame and cyclamate/saccharin blend as compared to sucrose at different concentrations. *Plant Foods for Human Nutrition*, vol. 54, pp. 119-130.

Cardoso, J.M.P., & Bolini, H.M.A. (2007). Different sweeteners in peach nectar: Ideal and equivalent sweetness. *Food Research International*, vol. 40, pp. 1249-1253.

Cooke, L. J. and Wardle, J. (2005). Age and gender differences in children's food preferences. *British Journal of Nutrition*. vol. 93, pp. 741-746.

Cox, D.N, Perry, I., Moore, P.B., Vallis, I., & Mela, D.J. (1999). Sensory and hedonic associations with macronutrient and energy intakes of lean and obese consumers. *International Journal of Obesity*, vol. 23, pp. 403-410.

Darwin, C. (1877). Biographiche skizze eines kleinen kindes. *Kosmos*, pp. 367-376.

Davis, C. Zai, C., Levitan, R.D., Kaplan, A.S., Carter, J.C., Reid-Westoby, C., Curtis, C., Wight, K., & Kennedy, J.L. (2011). Opiates, overeating and obesity: a psychogenetic analysis. *International Journal of Obesity*, vol. 35, pp. 1347-1354.

De Graaf, C., & Zandstra, E. H. (1999). Sweetness intensity and pleasantness in children, adolescents and adults. *Physiology and Behavior*, vol. 67, pp. 513-520.

Desor, J. A., & Beauchamp, G. K. (1987). Longitudinal Changes in Sweet Preferences in Humans. *Physiology and Behavior*, vol. 39, pp. 639-641.

Desor, J.A., Maller, O., & Turner, R.E. (1973). Taste in acceptance of sugars by human infants. *Journal of Comparative and Physiological Psychology*, vol. 84, pp. 496-501.

Drewnowski, A., Brunzell, A.J., Sande, K., Iverius, P.H., & Greenwood, M.R.C. (1985). Sweet tooth reconsidered: Taste responsiveness in human obesity. *Physiology and Behavior*, vol. 35, issue 4, pp. 617-622.

Drewnowski, A. (1997). Taste preferences and food intake. *Annual Review of Nutrition*, vol. 17, pp. 237-53.

Duffy, V.B., Peterson, J., Dinehart, M., & Bartoshuk, L.M. (2003). Genetic and environmental variation in taste: associations with sweet intensity, preference and intake. *Topics in Clinical Nutrition*, vol. 18, pp. 209-20.

Filozof, C., Gonzalez, C., Sereday, M., Mazza, C., and Braguinsky, J. (2001). Obesity prevalence and trends in Latin American countries. *Obesity Reviews*, vol. 2, pp. 99-106.

Glanville, E.V., Kaplan, A.R., & Fischer, R. (1964). Age Sex + Taste Sensitivity. *Journals of Gerontology*, vol. 19, issue 4, pp. 474-478.

Gibson, E.L., Wardle, J., & Watts, C.J. (1998). Fruit and vegetable consumption, nutritional knowledge and beliefs in mothers and children. *Appetite*, vol. 31, issue 2, pp. 205-228.

Holt, S.H.A., Cobiac, L., Beaumont-Smith, N.E., Easton, K., & Best, D.J. (2000). Dietary habits and the perception and liking of sweetness among Australian and Malaysian students: a cross-cultural study. *Food Quality and Preference*, vol. 11, pp. 299-312.

James, C.E., Laing, D.G., & Oram, N. (1997). A comparison of the ability of 8-9-year-old children and adults to detect taste stimuli. *Physiology & Behavior*, vol. 62, issue 1, pp. 193-197.

James, C.E., Laing, D.G., Jinks, A.L., Oram, N., & Hutchinson, I. (2004). Taste response functions of adults and children using different rating scales. *Food Quality and Preference*, vol. 15, issue 1, pp. 77-82.

Kildegaard, H. (2011). *Step-by-step changes of children's preferences towards healthier foods*. (Doctoral dissertation). Aarhus University, Aarhus.

Lawless, H.T. and Haymann, H. (2010). *Sensory Evaluation of Food*. New York: Springer Science + Business Media.

Liem, D.G., & de Graaf, C. (2004). Sweet and sour preference in young children and adults: role of repeated exposure. *Physiology & Behavior*, vol. 83, pp. 421-429.

Matsushita, Y., Mizoue, T., Takahashi, Y., Isogawa, A., Kato, M., Inoue, M., Noda, M., & Tsugane, S. (2009). Taste preferences and body weight change in Japanese adults: the JPHC study. *International Journal of Obesity*, vol. 33, pp. 1191-1197.

Mattes, R.D., and Mela, D.J. (1986). Relationships between and among selected measures of sweet taste preference and dietary intake. *Chemical. Senses*, vol. 11, pp. 523-39.

McCaughey, S.A. (2008). The taste of sugars. *Neuroscience and Biobehavioral Review*, vol. 32, pp. 1024-1043.

Meilgaard, M.C., Civille, G.V., & Carr, B.T. (2007). *Sensory Evaluation Techniques*. Boca Raton: CRC Press.

Mela, D.J. (1996). Eating behavior, food preferences and dietary intake in relation to obesity and body-weight status. *Proceedings of the Nutrition Society*, vol. 55, pp. 803-816.

Mela, D.J. (2001). Why do we like what we like? *Journal of the Science of Food and Agriculture*, vol. 81, issue 1, pp. 10-16.

Mojet, J., Christ-Hazelhof, E., & Heidema, J. (2001). Taste perception with age: Generic or specific losses in threshold sensitivity to the five basic tastes?. *Chemical Senses*, vol. 26, pp. 845-860.

Nicklaus, S., Boggio, V., Chabanet, C., & Issanchou, S. (2004). A prospective study of food preferences in childhood. *Food Quality and Preference*, vol. 15, pp. 805-818.

Nisbett, R.E., & Gurwitz, S.B. (1970). Weight, sex, and the eating behavior of human newborns. *Journal of Camparative and Physiological Psychology*, vol. 73, pp. 245-53.

Pangborn, R.M., & Giovanni, M.E. (1984). Dietary intake of sweet foods and of dairy fats and resultant gustatory responses to sugar in lemonade and to fat in milk. *Appetite*, vol. 5, pp. 317-327.

Reed, D.R., Bachmanov, A.A., Beauchamp, G.K., Tordoff, M.G., & Price, R.A. (1997). Heritable variation in food preferences and their contribution to obesity. *Behavior Genetics*, vol. 27, pp. 373-387.

Rodin, J., Moskowitz, H.R., and Bray, S.A. (1978). Relationship between obesity, weight loss, and taste responsiveness. *Physiology and Behavior*, vol. 17, pp. 391-397.

Salbe, A.D., Delparigi, A., Pratley, R.E., Drewnowski, A., & Tataranni, P. A. (2004). Taste preferences and body weight changes in an obesity-prone population. *Americal Journal of Clinical Nutrition*, vol. 79, pp. 372-378.

Sartor, F., Donaldson, L.F., Markland, D.A., Loveday, H., Jackson, M.J., & Kubis, H. (2011). Taste perception and implicit attitude toward sweet related to body mass index and soft drink supplementation. *Appetite*, vol. 57, issue 1, pp. 237-246.

Sharma, A., & Hedge, A.M. (2009). Relationship between body mass index, caries experience and dietary preferences in children. *Journal of Clinical Pediatric Dentistry*, vol. 34, pp. 49-52

Sherperd, R. (1989). Factors influencing food preference and choice. In R. Sherperd R. (Ed.), *Handbook of the psychophysiology of human eating*. New York: John Wiley & Sons Ltd.

Snyder, D.J., Duffy, V.B., Moskowitz, H., Hayes, J.E., & Bartoshunk, L.M. (2006). Revisiting the sweet tooth: Relationship between sweetness perception, sweet food preference, and BMI. *Chemical Senses*, A37.

Uauy, R., Albala, C., & Kain, J. (2001). Obesity trends in Latin America: Transiting from under- to overweight. *Journal of Nutrition*, vol. 131, pp. 893S-899S.

Zandstra, E.H., & de Graaf, C. (1998). Sensory perception and pleasantness of orange beverages from childhood to old age. *Food Quality and Preference*, vol. 9, issue 1-2, pp. 5-12.

CHAPTER III

Tasting Time: The Meaning of Sugar in Cuba. Contextualizing the Taste of Sweetness

By Susanne Højlund

A recent shift in opinion in health and nutrition sciences has transferred concerns about fat as a risky foodstuff onto sugar, which is now proposed to be a key risk factor for lifestyle diseases (see for example Taubes 2008). The possible correlation between sugar consumption and health problems, especially diabetes, obesity, and other lifestyle diseases, is an issue that is discussed worldwide. Often these health discourses are followed by universalistic statistics showing how much sugar we consume correlated with the incidence of diseases. The universalistic scientific knowledge of the body leads to the idea that it is the same factors that cause diseases such as diabetes and obesity everywhere. However, the statistical correlations do not explain why people eat sugar, and the biological explanations of the preference for sweetness are inadequate in isolation. Despite the fact that metabolism and other bodily functions seem to be rather stable and universal factors for health, understanding how certain conditions of the body are generated is impossible without grasping the local context of the problem (Lock & Nguyen 2010). The act of eating sugar and sweet foodstuffs has different meanings in different local contexts. In this article, I will argue that it is necessary to explore what sugar means to people before it is possible to give nutritional advice about how to consume it. With its focus on Cuba, this chapter is an example of such a contextualization. It investigates the Cuban context of sugar consumption through literature reviews and the results of small fieldwork projects conducted during four visits to Cuba between 2005 and 2011.[1]

THE CURRENT POLITICAL CONTEXT OF SUGAR

In the old streets of Havana, among dilapidated buildings and roads covered with mud and potholes, in a town which seems to lack all modern necessities, I was several times astonished to see people walking by with enormous cakes lifted up over their heads. I had to ask myself: what's going on? I did not see any bakeries displaying cakes or bread in their windows; to my western eyes, these cakes should have been expensive and rare treats, more for window-shopping than anything else, and I wondered how the average Cuban citizen could afford such a luxurious foodstuff. Once I had visited Cuba several times, I learned to interpret the scenery in relation to the Cuban context. Big, extravagant birthday cakes can perhaps be got very cheaply using your *libreta*, the food-rationing book that every Cuban receives from the state. I was also told that the cakes were not always available and were mostly for the special celebration of a fifteenth birthday. But if you were able to pay with *Pesos Convertibles* the situation was different: you had access to more shops, more varied foods, and could be more confident that you would be able to serve the traditional cake at your child's next birthday. This is just one small example of the fact that in Cuba, eating is not just eating. Buying and preparing food, and cooking and maintaining culinary traditions, are complicated processes deeply dependent on the country's political situation and intertwined with its history, especially of sugar production.

While sugar production and consumption are increasing in the Latin American region, especially in Brazil, the opposite is the case in Cuba. In fact Brazil has replaced Cuba as the world's biggest sugar producer. The production of sugar has a special history in Cuba; since the late 1800s, it had been a dominant producer on the world market right up until a dramatic

---

1   I want to thank ICAP for arranging stimulating and informative visits at different institutions in 2007, Henrik Theil Hansen and his family for sharing his knowledge about everyday life in Cuba, our many Cuban friends for hospitality and street level introductions to Cuba, dr. Vanessa Vásquez and Dr. Antonio J. Martinez Fuentes Universidad de la Habana for inspiring dialogues and for making it possible to present the Sugar and Modernity project at the International conference Anthropos 2011, and the Cuban ambassador in Denmark, Guillermo Vázquez Moreno, for showing interest in our project during his visit at Aarhus University, in 2009.

change occurred in a very short period between 1991 and 1994. At this time production was halved and many sugar mills closed, causing massive unemployment. This sudden and rather catastrophic change was a consequence of the fall of the Soviet Union: Cuba lost its most important markets and trade partners regarding the export of sugar and the import of other items, especially oil. Within three years the country lost 70% of its import capacity, a development that brought Cuba officially to ascribe sugar a new position in the state economy (Chomsky, Carr, & Smorkaloff 2003: 595; Peters 2008; Pollit 2004; Hagelberg & Alvarez 2005, see also Simonsen, this book). The so-called "Special Period" declared by Fidel Castro following the fall of Soviet Union is still on-going, as the Cubans experience a lack of all kinds of goods, and especially in the beginning of the period also poverty, hunger, and depression – in addition to the US embargo. In relation to the decline of the sugar exports, in 2002 a restructuring plan was introduced that changed sugar production again, closing many more sugar mills and supporting the former sugar workers in their efforts to get re-educated in order to find new jobs (Pollit 2004: 331).

But the fact that sugar production declined so dramatically that the Cuban economy nearly broke down caused another industry to grow, with crucial consequences for the Cuban society, namely tourism (Jiménez 2008). As part of its plan for economic recovery, the Cuban government focused on tourism as a new resource of income; the tourist became the new commodity that could stabilize the economy. Where before sugar had been Cuba's primary link to the global society, that role was now played by tourism. This meant some more liberal strategies had to be tolerated. Tourism is not controlled by a politically regulated state market in the same way as sugar production was, and it is now possible for the ordinary Cuban to make money from tourists, for example by putting up a kind of hotel room in one's own house, known as a "Casa Particulare" – though this is subject to heavy taxation. The biggest impact of the tourism strategy was caused by the temporary admission of US dollars into the country, which stimulated a double economy, splitting up the population into those who worked with tourists and those who did not: in other words, those who had access to US dollars and dollar shops and those who did not. This development is well-known, and it is also well-known that the tourism strategy failed to solve the social problems caused by the decline in income from the sugar industry (Jiménez 2008; Wilson 2009). The political ideal of equality was and is threatened, and Cuba is now facing the problems of inequality, including increases in crime, social problems, and social conflicts. The US dollar has now been forbidden again, but there is still a double economy created by the division between *pesos convertible* and Cuban pesos. *Pesos convertible* (for tourists) are worth more than twenty times as much as Cuban pesos.

"No es facil" (it is not easy) has become an everyday phrase in daily conversation since the beginning of the Special Period in Cuba. The saying is often used in the context of the everyday problems of lack – of food, work, clothes, electricity, and jobs – or when facing the problems of the double economy and the negative consequences of tourism.

SUGAR AND HEALTH

The Special Period has also been an enormous challenge for the country in terms of the health of the population. Aside from the struggle initiated by the US blockade, the breakdown of the sugar industry added new problems. Sudden rises in unemployment, economic depression, and a lack of all kinds of goods created a *nutritional transition* (Popkin 2001) that within a short time brought severe deficiency diseases with it (Rodriguez-Ojea et al. 2002; Brenner et al. 2008; Brotherton 2012). The average diet changed rapidly, with energy from sugar cane and carbohydrates increasing percentage-wise in relation to the intake of protein and fat. This resulted in a general *loss* of weight in the population and a correspondent decrease in coronary diseases and diabetes – a 'natural experiment' which demands international interest (ibid.; see also Franco 2007, 2008). The fact that in 1991 Cuba was consuming more sugar per capita than any other country in the world (Amador & Pera 1991), and at the same time experienced a decrease in the so-called lifestyle diseases destabilizes the idea of a direct connection between sugar consumption and these diseases.

Twenty years on, these diseases have become a huge problem in Cuban society, as is the case across the world. For example, rates of diabetes are expected to double three times before 2030 (Wild et al. 2004; Osa 2010), and obesity is also a growing problem (Menéndez & Acosta 2005; Farinas et al. 2011). According to the Cuban newspaper *Granma* a special programme is currently being engineered to help solve these issues (Osa 2010). In spite of these challenges, Cuba is still the country in Latin America with the healthiest population: undernourishment is now low (Ziegler et al. 2011), life expectancy high (approximately 76), and infant mortality low (Brotherton 2012: 19). Cuba is proud of its free health care system, but the necessary medicines are always scarce (ibid.).

The level of knowledge and information about health among the population is in general very high, probably as a result of the ideal of education, which is very strong in Cuba (see also Brotherton 2012: 57). Television plays a key role in daily communication and education. Even tiny schools far away from the capital city have televisions, and much of the school curriculum and teaching are based on educational TV programmes. Nearly 70% of all broadcasting in Cuba has an educational purpose, including information about health:[2] *Hablemos de la salud* ("Let's talk about health") is broadcasted once a week. The damaging impact of smoking is an example of an issue addressed by this programme, but it also broadcasts debates about the official health recommendations and prevention politics. Another example of this kind of programme is *Vale la pena* ("It is worth it"), where once a week you can send in questions and get answers from a psychologist. There is also a brief daily information programme that has health-related themes, and a programme called *Exacta* ("The correct doses"), which explains the correct doses of different medicines. Medicine is nearly free in Cuba, which means that people have many different more or less useful medicines at home, and often try to regulate it themselves. *Exacta* communicates knowledge about specific diseases and uses actors as well as medical specialists. On the radio, there is a daily programme called *Por nuestros campos y ciudades* ("Through our land and cities"), which is about different kind of diseases, and in the official newspaper of the government *Granma* there are often articles about health and illness, as well as reports from the many Cuban doctors abroad. Cuba has at least 25,000 doctors carrying out voluntary work in other countries at any one time, and people are in general very knowledgeable about and proud of the work of these doctors, who are seen as symbols of the revolution (Brotherton 2012: 59, 83).

Access to doctors is very easy in Cuba as every family has its own family doctor, often living in the same street. One doctor has typically around 650 patients – compared to the situation in Scandinavia, this is a very small number. In the media people are encouraged to use their family doctor, and the saying "Prevention before cure" is often mentioned. Sugar is not an explicit issue in these media discourses, unlike in Denmark for example, where there is currently much focus on sugar as an evil element in our diet (Højlund 2011).

Health problems that are understood to be lifestyle-related are, as mentioned above, common in Cuba today as well as in other parts of Latin Amer-

---

2   Examples are from 2009.

ica. But while sugar consumption in other parts of the world is increasing, this is to my knowledge not possible to determine in Cuba. Sugar is part of the state-driven food supply, and is not available on a free market; every household receives 10lbs (4,5 kilos) of sugar every month from the state at very little cost. Thus the amount of sugar each citizen has at his disposal is to a certain degree controlled and has not increased in recent years, although it is difficult to get identical reports about the exact ration, and sugar is probably also part of the informal exchange system (Rosendal 1997; Ziegler 2011; Alvarez 2004; Garth 2009; Wilson 2009).

In comparisons of sugar consumption and population health in different countries in Latin America Cuba stands out. In Brazil, for example, production and consumption of sugar are increasing at the same speed as rates of diabetes and obesity, and in general those countries worldwide that have the highest consumption of sugar also have the most incidences of diabetes.[3] It is tempting to conclude from these statistics that the more sugar you eat the less healthy you become. But this correlation is not as obvious in a Cuban context, where the beginning of the Special Period saw a remarkable simultaneity of increased sugar (carbohydrate) consumption and a decrease in lifestyle diseases, and where today it is difficult to document a relationship between the growing rates of diabetes and obesity and any similar increase in sugar consumption. Though Cubans traditionally have eaten a lot of sugar this does not explain why diabetes and obesity rates are increasing right now, as they are elsewhere in the world.

The lesson we can learn from this example is that statistics and macro approaches to health, history, and economics can be insufficient when used as the only parameters to explain a certain development. In order to shed light on the correlation between sugar and health, it is necessary to supplement the metadata with an understanding at a social and cultural level. McDaniels, who studied health promotion in Havana, used the phrase "social construction of risk" to refer to the notion that how a society collectively defines and responds to a given hazard is determined by social discourse, not merely by science or technological information (McDaniels 1998). In other words, if we are to understand the role of sugar for health, and to give nutritional advice on the subject, it is important for us to focus on local perceptions and uses of sugar.

---

3   P.B. Jeppesen, personal communication, March 8, 2010, see also Jeppesen, chapter 1, this book.

> Sugar seems not only good to eat, but good to think, not only metabolic but metaphoric, not only sucrose, but symbol. (Knight 2009: 201, with reference to Errington & Gewertz 2004: 54).

Sugar is many things: molecules (glucose, fructose, lactose etc.), a foodstuff (such as sugar cane or sugar beet), nutrition (carbohydrates, calories), a commodity (e.g. white and brown sugar or corn syrup) – but it also refers to the taste of sweetness (Ahmed et al. 2001). Sugar represents a materiality, whereas taste is a sensation – but how can we differentiate the two or analyze their interconnectedness?

Through his many analyses of sugar from a historical perspective, Sidney Mintz has shown how the preference for sweetness can be explained as a social construction (Mintz 1985, 1996). To Mintz the demand for sweetness is not a natural demand, but determined by historical processes related to early sugar production in the Caribbean. The question is how this "demand" is transformed into the ritual of daily necessity (ibid). He proposes that it happens through the symbolic meanings sugar has obtained through history. It is this symbolism that is interesting for our understanding of how the demand for sweetness has become part of modern lifestyles. Many writers have analyzed the variety of symbolic meanings represented by sugar, as an image of pleasure (Richardson 2002); as a figure for social values (James 1990); as part of risk taking (Lupton 1996); and as a sign for negative moral meanings (Rozin 1997). Sugar is thus loaded with significations that are often paradoxical and can give rise to ambivalence: it is good for your taste buds but bad for your health (Fischler 1987). But how do these symbolic meanings influence daily culinary practices? How does an idea about sugar lead to eating or not eating sugar? I propose that the many meanings of sugar make it necessary for us to pay close attention to taste itself, and more precisely to how a certain taste forms part of a culinary context.

Discussions of taste are often formulated as a relationship between a subject and a product. In the approach of the natural sciences, taste is about the physiological relation between a human being and a material substance. It is often stated as regards the preference for sweetness that this is something human beings are born with due to the baby's early experience of breast milk (Macbeth 1997; see also Kidmose, this volume). The sociological approach is also about a relation between a human being and a thing, since it understands taste as a sign of social differentiation and states that attraction towards certain things represents your social identity. Here an explanation of the preference for sweetness will be linked to your social position or habits; you are attracted to the thing because of your social status (Bourdieu 1984). Teil and Hennion (2004) combine the two approaches and encourage us to study them in one analytical manoeuvre, so that neither the scientific nor the sociological approach has priority.

Taste is not simply a property of a substance, nor is it a human competence; it is neither an individual perception nor a certain quality of a product, but a practice that generates social collectives and connects you to things and to other people. You are performing taste, Teil and Hennion argue, like wine tasters or guests at a gourmet restaurant. Daily life has its own "taste collectives", which transform the quality of the material foodstuff to the social, and vice versa (Teil & Hennion 2004). Adding sugar to your coffee, eating ice cream or birthday cake, and drinking sweet drinks are all cultural performances, much more than the simple matter of physiology and bodily sensations. The baby's tasting of its mother's milk is thus about being part of a taste collective, where sugar and human relationships are knit together as senses are culturally moulded (see also Falk 1991).

This definition inspires us to see sugar consumption and the taste of sweetness as parts of an integrated social practice that unify people or create taste collectives. It is thus important here to ask how Cubaness, sugar, and sweetness are related.

SUGAR CONSUMPTION IN EVERYDAY LIFE

I prefer my coffee without sugar. Normally this habit is not object of self-reflection, as many other Danes drink their coffee this way. During my four visits to Cuba, however, I was offered many cups of very sugary coffee by the kind hosts where we lived; when I asked for coffee without sugar I was always met with suspicion and astonishment, some laughter and many comments about my strange habit. Travelling to Cuba made my sweet or not-sweet tooth explicit and made me aware of taste as a cultural phenomenon. Crossing geographical borders is thus also about crossing culinary borders, travelling to other foodscapes and food traditions. This is obvious knowledge for any tourist, fieldworker, or businessman; even the sugar industry knows that sweet products should be produced in order to match local preferences for sweetness. But for the insider, taste preferences are seldom reflected on or problematical.

Every culture has its taste preferences, its core products, and its national cuisine (Belasco 2008). In Cuba, the national cuisine is characterized by a high uniformity in taste (Paponnet-Cantat 2003). Though it has its roots in Asian, Spanish, African, and North American culinary traditions, the variety of spices and food ingredients used is minimal (ibid.). The 50-year-plus US trade blockade against Cuba and the Special Period of the last 20 years has not made it easy for Cuban food lovers, cooks, and housewives to be creative in the kitchen and develop new recipes. Rice, black beans, eggs, fish, chicken, fruit, and avocados have for a long time been the main elements of all Cuban menus. The negative consequences of the scarcity of food have been reduced through the food rationing system, which was established in 1962 (Alvaréz 2004). This gives every Cuban citizen access to very cheap food items such as bread, rice, and meat; however, many of these food items are not always available (Garth 2009; Alvarez 2004; Wilson 2009). The only commodity available with any reliability over the last 20 years has been sugar.

The food programme also secures daily meals for schools, institutions, and work places, distributing an enormous number of meals every day (Alvarez 2004).[4] Although the programme is often mentioned with pride as having prevented malnutrition and secured food for every part of the population, many Cubans are tired of the monotonous taste of the programme, as well as the difficulties of getting all the foodstuffs they are promised in the *libreta* (Wilson 2009; Garth 2009; Henken 2008).

Though Cubans have no access to spices and no tradition of making spicy food, they love the taste of sweetness. Sweet food is constantly available and a fast way to forget that you are hungry. As a local citizen you know which window to pass in order to buy (more or less legally) homemade cookies and ice cream, or where the baker works and how to get a slice of cake from the bakery to tame your appetite. If you walking in the streets of Havana and happen to be invited to a religious celebration in a private home, you can be sure you will be offered a piece of cake. A first date should take place at Coppelia's, where they serve cheap and delightful ice cream. Even riding in the mountains with a local tourist guide, passing a field of sugar canes can rescue you from the unpleasant feeling of low blood sugar. The sugar-based Sunday rum shared with friends is a must (Wilson 2009) and a mojito without sugar is not a mojito. Sugar is also a necessity in the many homemade fresh fruit juices, and a sweet dessert – often a rice pudding – is part of the everyday school meal.

---

4   In 1991 it was more than 3 million a day, according to a UN report.

It seems that Cubans have an easy relationship with sugar: it is not one of the items that are always scarce, and there is an absence of moral panic regarding the consumption of sugar – it is just something that is there, and is not in general perceived as dangerous to one's health. Besides, a healthy body should not be too thin: a real husband should have a good stomach, I was told, since it shows that he has been able to create a good life for himself and his family. The easy access to sugar and the preference for sweetness makes it natural that events and celebrations always include cakes. The birthday cake with its luxurious appearance, its ability to gather people together, to make a party where the taste of sweetness is shared, is a welcome relief from the everyday experience of "No-es-facil".

GENERATIONAL DIFFERENCES IN RELATIONSHIPS WITH SUGAR

To eat sugar, not only for pleasure, but also as a strategy for coping with hunger is a practice which lies deeply rooted in Cuban everyday life. "When you say sugar I come to think of my childhood, when we had to drink a glass of warm sugar cane juice in order to keep our hunger away." This statement – and it was not a sweet memory – was expressed by a Cuban colleague I met at a conference; it points to how historical moments are part of the experience of taste. There is a collective practice behind this memory; it was a normal way of coping with hunger (see e.g. Brenner et al. 2008). The memory of hunger refers to a precise period in Cuban history, the early years of the Special Period. Sugar cane was the core product of Cuba until the fall of the wall in 1989, and you can still buy juice pressed from the sugar cane at cottages on the roadside.

With this example I want to draw attention to the close link between taste and memory. Food has the ability to form and maintain a historical consciousness (Sutton 2001). Christiane Paponett-Cantat and Hanna Garth, who both did fieldwork in Cuba studying food practices, have illustrated this with their ethnographic examples of how Cuban narratives of food are linked to historical moments (Garth 2009; Paponnet-Cantat 2003). There were certain periods – especially before and after the revolution and before and after the beginning of the Special Period – when foods were ascribed certain meanings, so that those foods remind people of differences in food choice and taste, different conditions that existed for access to food, and different possibilities for variations in taste experiences. For the studies' informants, milk or cornflakes, tomatoes or spices were linked to memories either of better times or harder times in general.

Along the road you can still buy hand presssed, fresh sugarcane juice. Photo: Susanne Højlund, 2010

Giovanna Neri argues in another ethnographical food study conducted in Havana that young people position themselves by expressing distance from the national food programme and instead seek status by eating and drinking food not distributed through the *libreta*. Drinking Cola seems to be a very particular sign of status among young people in the streets of Havana (Neri 2010), who are dreaming of a better future and – perhaps inspired by the many tourists and the modern ideal of globalization – are curious to explore the world outside Cuba. There is no doubt that this demographic or generational taste collective will be a target group for the food market that is expected to grow in Cuba over the coming years (Alvarez 2004a), and thereby influence the role the cultural taste of sweetness will play in the future. As stated by Henriksen (this volume), Coca-Cola is a strong brand for these visions. These young people will tell different stories about food and the meaning of sugar from the elder generation. Certain foods and tastes remind you of your place in history.

Studying Cuba through the lens of sugar reveals the multifaceted meanings this product has had and still has for the everyday life of Cuba. The country's multi-ethnic population, its history of slavery and social life in the sugar mills, its time under Batista, its production (and consumption) of rum, its incredible musical culture, its economic situation, its everyday life, and the changes it experienced before and after the breakdown of the Soviet Union are all components of Cuban culture that can be related to sugar (Catauro 2005). Sugar is thus a foodstuff deeply related to Cuban identity, as is also reflected in the local saying "Sin Azúcar no hay País" ("without sugar there is no country") or in the famous book by Fernando Ortiz, where sugar and tobacco are used as metaphors to describe the mixed Cuban culture and the process of "transculturation" (Ortiz 2003). Today people from other parts of the world come to the island not to work in (though perhaps to learn about) the sugar plantations, but to enjoy the culture, the weather, and the landscape, and to study the interesting history of the island. The deep interconnection between the people and the sugar cane will change its cultural value, and the saying "Sin Azúcar no hay Pais" will perhaps be reformulated in another direction: "Sin Azúcar tambien hay Pais" ("without sugar there is also a country").

SUGAR, MODERNITY, AND TIME

The commonly accepted cause of diabetes and obesity is the so-called modern lifestyle. However, in Cuba lifestyles are not explicitly formulated as health risks in the many health programmes (Brotherton 2012: 113) and the absence of a health morality in relation to sugar does not make it easier to include high sugar consumption as part of a lifestyle risk parameter. It is therefore a question whether there is any sense in linking modern lifestyle diseases and sugar intake in Cuba. In addition, the concept of a "modern lifestyle" is analytically a big black box, containing everything from low levels of physical activity to consumption of fast food, busy work lives, stress, computers, consumerism, and urbanization. Perhaps this complexity of meaning stems from the blurred meaning of "modernity" as a concept.

Modernity is both an empirical and a theoretical concept, and it refers to development as well as to a time period, industrialization, modernization, knowledge, universalism, rationality, and a decline in religious beliefs in favour of scientific ideas. Modernity can be thought of in the singular or we can use it to represent multiple modernities. It is often seen as a European project, though it is also argued that the Caribbean was modern before Europe (Cooper 2005; Scott 2004). Modernity is thus a multifaceted analytical concept and therefore has little conceptual power in itself (Wade 2007). Perhaps it is better to state that when you say something about modernity, you say something about *time* (Cooper 2005). From an anthropological perspective, the task is therefore "to be sensitive to the different ways people frame the relationship of past, present and future" (ibid.: 149). To Cooper there would be no such a phenomenon as a modern lifestyle in itself, but there could be an *idea* of a style or way of living that is embedded in perceptions of time. If we want to understand what the local meanings of sugar and sweetness are time is thus a central concept.

I have tried to show how the cultural sense of sweetness is a historical taste related to and experienced in certain taste collectives. Age and generation can define these collectives, but others – for example those of the family collective – will have other sugar memories to share. For certain taste collectives in Cuba with identities that are strongly associated with the past, sugar and sweetness recall memories of difficult times. But we should also look into what sugar means for a modern lifestyle today. It could be interesting to explore how sugar and sweetness also represents futurity and points to particular aspirations in Cuba.

CONCLUSION

The Cuban example of atypical statistics regarding the relation between sugar consumption and diabetes/obesity points to a need for more contextualized analyses. The case has not been studied in enough depth to counter the common perception of the role of sugar for health, and it is doubtful whether the statistics can provide any answers at all. My contribution to this debate takes a sociocultural approach, studying sugar culture and trying to understand how sugar finds its way into people's daily meals. Rather than attempting to find proofs for the existence or non-existence of a relation between sugar consumption and health, I am arguing for an ethnographic approach to modernity – deconstructing lifestyle, modernity, and sugar, and exploring the everyday life of the Cuban consumer. For this approach it is important to place the taste of sweetness in time, and not only explore the past, its memories and history, but also the future, investigating how sugar represents a feeling of novelty. Sugar is no longer associated with ideas of authenticity, or traditional ideas of it as a national core product: images of big fields of sugar canes, richness, a sweet life, or of hunger and a daily struggle for food are long gone – also it is now connected to ideas of change, globalization, and a better life. Different generations of the Cuban population will probably interpret the changes in society caused by the dramatic history of sugar differently.

But in spite of the structural changes that occurred in Cuba on account of sugar, the demand for products with a sweet taste has not been diminished.

Sweetness is still a big part of the national cuisine and sugar still will find a way to satisfy this demand, perhaps now through associations with ideas of a new lifestyle, with (Coca-) cola in particular as a strong symbol for youth and aspiration (Foster 2008). This specific age group symbolizes the future in many ways, and it also represents a new consumer category in Cuban society, I assume. The product behind this demand is not the sugar cane anymore, but more industrialized (and hidden) versions of sugar, as for example the High Fructose Corn Syrup used in many sweetened products and soft drinks, or different processed versions of the stevia plant. These are commodities of sweetness which will certainly find their way onto the Cuban market during the ongoing process of liberalization and increased trade with other countries. What this means for taste, lifestyle, and health is another question for research.

BIBLIOGRAPHY

Ahmed, Z, et al. (2001). Concept of sugar – A review. *OnLine Journal of Biological Sciences*, vol. 1, issue 9, pp. 883-894. Asian Network for Scientific Information.

Alvarez, J. (2004a). Overview of Cuba's food rationing system. University of Florida, IFAS. FE482

Alvarez, J. (2004b).The issue of food security in Cuba. University of Florida, IFAS. FE483

Amador, M., & Pera, M. (1991). Nutrition and health issues in Cuba: Strategies for a developing country. *Report, Food and Nutrition Bulletin*, vol. 13, issue 4. UN Report.

Belasco, W. (2008). *Food. The Key Concepts*. Oxford: Berg.

Bourdieu, P. (1984). *Distinction. A Social Critique of the Judgement of Taste*. Cambridge: Harvard University Press.

Brenner, P et al. (2008). *A Contemporary Cuba Reader. Reinventing the Revolution*. Lanham: Rowman & Littlefield Publishers, Inc.

Brotherton, S. P. (2012). *Revolutionary Medicine. Health and the Body in Post-Soviet Cuba*. Durham and London: Duke University Press.

Catauro. (2005). *Revista Cubana de Antropología*, vol. 6, issue 11.

Chomsky, A., Carr, B. & Smorkaloff, P. M. (Eds.) (2003). *The Cuban Reader. History, Culture, Politics*. Durham, London: Duke University Press.

Cooper, F. (2005). Modernity. In *Colonialism in Question. Theory, Knowledge, History*. London: University of California Press.

Errington, F. & Gewertz, D. (2004). *Yali's Question: Sugar, Culture and History*. Chicago: Chicago University Press.

Falk, P. (1991). Homo Culinarius: towards an historical anthropology of taste. *Social Science Information*, vol. 30, p 757-790. SAGE.

Fariñas, L. et al. (2011). Prevalencia de sobrepeso y obesidad en nonos de 6 a 11 años del reparto fontanar. Memorias Convención Internacional de Antropología: Anthropos 2011. II Congreso Iberoamericano de Antropología. CD: 978-959-7091-77-6. 2986-3001.

Fischler, C. (1987). Attitudes towards sugar and sweetness in historical and social perspective. In J. Dobbing (ed.), *Sweetness*. Heidelberg: Springer Verlag, pp. 83-99.

Foster, R.J. (2008). *Coca-Globalization. Following Soft Drinks from New York to New Guinea.* Houndsmill. Basingstoke: Palgrave Macmillian.

Franco, M. et al. (2007). Impact of energy intake, physical activity and population-wide weight loss on cardiovascular disease and diabetes mortality in Cuba, 1980-2005. *American Journal of Epidmiology*, vol. 166, issue 12, pp. 1374-1380.

Franco, M. et al. (2008). Obesity reduction and its possible consequences: What can we learn from the "Special Period" in Cuba? *Canadian Medical Association Journal*, vol. 178, issue 8, pp. 1032-1034.

Garth, H. (2009). Things became scarce: food availability and accessibility in Santiago de Cuba then and now. *NAPA Bulletin*, vol. 32, pp. 178-192.

Hagelberg, G.B., & Alvarz, J. (2005). Historical Overview of Cuba's Costs of Sugar Production. University of Florida, IFAS Extension, paper FE626.

Henken, T. (2008). Vale Todos: In Cuba's Paladares, everything is prohibited but anything goes. In Brenner, P et al.: *A Contemporary Cuba Reader. Reinventing the Revolution.* Lanham: Rowman & Littlefield Publishers, Inc.

Højlund, S. og Koustrup, L. (2011). Sukkerdjævelen: om dæmonisering af smag, moralsk panik og pædagogik. *Jordens Folk*, vol. 46, Issue 4, pp. 12-18.

James, A. (1990). The good, the bad and the delicious: the role of confectionery in British society. *The Sociological Review*, vol. 38, issue 4, pp. 666-688.

Jiménez, M.R. (2008). The political economy of leisure. In P. Brenner et al. (Eds.), *A Contemporary Cuba Reader. Reinventing the Revolution.* Lanham: Rowman & Littlefield Publishers, Inc.

Knight, G.R. (2009). A house of honey: White sugar, brown sugar, and the taste for modernity in colonial and postcolonial Indonesia. *Food and Foodways*, vol. 17, pp. 197-214.

Lock, M. & Nguyen, V.-K. (2010). *An Anthropology of Biomedicine.* West Sussex: Wiley-Blackwell.

Lupton, D. (1996). *Food, the Body and the Self.* London: SAGE Publications.

McDaniels, T.L. cited in Tate et al. (2003). *Health Promotion International*, vol. 18, issue 4, pp. 279-286.

Macbeth, H. (Ed.) (1997). *Food Preferences and Taste: Continuity and Change.* Berghan Books Series: The Anthropology of Food and Nutrition. Oxford: Berghan Books.

Menéndez, A.R.-O., & Acosta, S.J. (2005). Is obesity a health problem in Cuba? In K. Bose (Ed.), Human Obesity: A Major Health Problem [Special Issue]. *Human Ecology*, vol. 13, pp. 115-119.

Mintz, S. (1985). *Sweetness and Power. The Place of Sugar in Modern History.* London: Penguin Books.

Mintz, S. (1996). *Tasting Food, Tasting Freedom. Excursions into Eating, Culture and the Past.* Boston: Beacon Press.

Neri, G. (2010). State food or status food? Notes on food and imagination policies in Ciudad de la Habana. (Unpublished conference paper given at the European Association of Social Anthropologists conference, Maynooth University, Ireland).

Ortiz, F. (1995). *Cuban Counterpoint. Tobacco and Sugar.* Durham and London: Duke University Press.

de la Osa, J. A. (2010, November 10). Uno de cada 22 cubanos padece diabetes mellitus. *Granma*.

Papponet-Cantat, C.N. (2003). The Joy of Eating: Food and Identity in Contemporary Cuba. *Caribbean Quarterly*, vol. 49, issue 3, pp. 11-29.

Peters, P. (2008). Cutting losses: Cuba downsizes its sugar industry. In P. Brenner et al. (Eds.), *Reinventing the Revolution. A Contemporary Cuba Reader.* New York: Rowman & Littlefield Publishers Inc.

Pollit, B.H. (2004). The rise and fall of the Cuban sugar economy. *Journal of Latin American Studies*, vol. 36, issue 2, pp. 319-348.

Popkin, B.M. (2001). The nutrition transition and obesity in the developing world. *Journal of Nutrition*, vol. 131, pp. 871S-873S.

Richardson, T. (2002). *Sweets. A* History *of Temptation*. London: Bantam Press.

Rodriguez-Ojea,A. et al (2002). The nutrition transition in Cuba in the nineties: an overview. *Public Health Nutrition*, vol. 5, 1A, pp. 129-133.

Rosendahl, M. (1997). *Inside the Revolution. Everyday Life in Socialist Cuba.* Ithaca, London: Cornell University Press.

Rozin, P. (1987). Sweetness, sensuality, sin, safety, and socialization: Some speculations. In J. Dobbing (Ed.), *Sweetness.* Heidelberg: Springer Verlag.

Scott, D. (2004). Modernity that predated the modern: Sidney Mintz's Caribbean.*History Workshop Journal*, issue 58, pp. 191-210.

Sutton, D.E. (2001). *Remembrance of Repasts: An Anthropology of Food and Memory.* Oxford: Berg.

Taube, G. (2008). *Good Calories, Bad Calories. Fats, Carbs and the Controversial Science of Diet and Health.* New York: Anchor Books.

Teil, G., & Hennion, A. (2004). Discovering quality or performing taste? A sociology of the amateur. In H. Mark (Ed.), *Qualities of Food.* Manchester: Manchester University Press.

Wade, P. (2007). Modernity and tradition. Shifting boundaries, shifting contexts. In N. Miller, & S. Hart (Eds.), *When was Latin America Modern?* Studies of the Americas. London: Palgrave Macmillan.

Wild, S. et al. (2004): Global prevalence of diabetes: estimates for the year 2000 and projections for 2030. *Diabetes Care*, vol. 27, issue 5, pp. 1047-1053.

Wilson, Marisa. 2009. Food as a good vs. food as a commodity: contradictions between state and market in Tuta, Cuba. *Journal of the Anthropological Society of Oxford (JASO)*, N.S. vol. 1,issue 1, pp. 25-51.

Woloson, W.A. (2002). *Refined Tastes. Sugar, Confectionery, and Consumers in Nineteenth-Century America.* Baltimore, London: Johns Hopkins University Press.

Ziegler, J., Goay, C., Mahon, C., & Way, S.-A. (2011). Cuba. In Ziegler, J. et al. (Eds.), *The Fight for the Right to Food. Lessons Learned*, pp. 310-331. International Relations and Development Series. Geneva: The Graduate Institute, Geneva Publications.

PART THREE: THE GLOCALIZED PRACTICES

Opening Remarks

By Ken Henriksen

Sometimes coincidences help clarify complicated matters. I had just started writing this short introduction when surprising news broke about some recent legislation in Uruguay. In this largely Roman Catholic South American country that suffers from high levels of poverty and inequality, the government has recently enforced rules for the production and distribution of marijuana (on August 5, 2013). This happens at a time when the legalization of marijuana is being discussed by the public as well as by legislative bodies in several Latin American countries. The legalization of drugs is undoubtedly a contested and controversial issue with large numbers of opponents all over the world. But whether we are proponents or opponents, it reminds us that in Latin America there is perhaps a sometimes exaggerated movement toward the secularization and rationalization of cultural and political life. More than anything else, the idea of the world as one that is open to transformation and modernization has become common sense in many parts of the region.

In many Latin American countries, abortion has been legalized, same-sex marriage laws passed, and today anti-discrimination laws are widespread. During the era of democratic transition in the 1990s and at the beginning of this century, modern democratic values were enshrined within new constitutions, giving indigenous groups the rights and recognition that had been ignored or violated for centuries (as noted in Oehlerich's article in this volume). As a result, autonomous regimes have been introduced and universities that teach curricula in indigenous languages established. Moreover, in most of these countries an accelerated process of urbanization has resulted in the rise of modern cities with complicated infrastructures and metropolitan symbols of modernity such as sophisticated business quarters and skyscrapers.

Outside of the metropolis, sugar cane farms are undergoing rapid processes of modernization in order to meet the demands for sugar that are in part a result of growing rates of consumption of sugar amongst all population groups. However, sugar cane is today also used for the production of ethanol fuel, which is widely used in Brazil. For these and many other reasons, large amounts of money in Brazil and other Latin American countries are invested in research and development with the aim of fabricating genetically modified sugar cane species that are adapted to changing weather conditions and resistant to diseases. Still, given the large numbers of small or medium-sized producers with limited resources for investment in modern technologies, many producers have to rely on traditional production and harvest methods.

It is therefore undeniable, as Canclini has written, "that Latin America has modernized, as a society and as a culture" (2001: 64). But, as he adds, it is a modernization that has resulted in high levels of inequality and uneven access to its symbolic goods (2001: 65). Global trends such as the focus on healthy lifestyles with low-calorie foods and frequent exercise have also reached Latin America. However, at the same time, dramatic increases in rates of obesity and diabetes, especially among the poorest segments of the population, remain one among many indications of a region experiencing varying forms of modernity.

It would be a mistake to deny the dark sides of modernity that have evolved in urban areas in most parts of Latin America. Besides health problems, it is needless to mention the poor and often informal neighbourhoods such as the *favelas* in Brazil, and other urban areas haunted by poverty and crime, or ruled by illegal drugs gangs. Such problems should not been seen as the remnants of the past. Instead they remind us that modernity is always plural, and that we need to study how the modern is always localized and embedded in local practices.

Putting emphasis on sacrificial rituals in which sugar or sugar-rich goods play a crucial role, two of the chapters in this section cast light on specific variations of modernity in Bolivia and Mexico. They show us that sugar, and sugar-rich goods such as Coca-Cola, has *democratized*, filtering down to even the poorest communities. Through rituals and other locally embedded practices, these goods are appropriated and thereby re-shaped into new hybrid forms. Modernity, it is argued, can therefore best be understood if we study the ways in which it becomes significant to local communities.

The contribution by Bjoern and Kidmose is an investigation of the relationship between changing production and harvest methods in Brazil and the quality of sugar cane yields. They show how recent legislation in this country, which produces more sugar cane than any other country in the world, has contributed to the modernization of the sector. Despite the large number of small farmers, especially in the Rio de Janeiro area, the results are improved quality and higher yields.

CHAPTER IV

Estás Aquí Para Ser Feliz:
The Globalization of Sweetened
Soft Drinks in Mexico

By Ken Henriksen

Sweetened soft drinks have become an important economic and cultural commodity in most parts of Latin America, and Mexico is today one of the largest consumers of Coca-Cola per capita in the world.[1] Many studies show that this trend is part of a general change in consumption patterns involving a greater intake of sugar-rich and low-nutrient products (Rivera et al. 2008). Such foods and drinks were once unavailable in both urban and rural areas of Mexico, but in the cities they can now be purchased in modern super-markets. In rural communities, where reliance on locally based production systems is often in decline, there is easy access to canned foods, soft drinks, and snack foods in small shops located on every street corner. For many years, Coca-Cola's slogan was "an arm's length from desire," which refers to the goal of making the drink available at every corner of even the remotest village (Pendergast 2000; Leatherman & Goodman 2005). There is significant evidence to suggest that the company has been successful in achieving this goal. It is easier in both rural and urban areas of Mexico to get a soft drink than a glass of clean water; the vast majority of Mexico City's public schools, for example, lack potable water.

The socioeconomic context of this development is beyond any doubt the

---

[1]   According to the Coca-Cola Company's own statistics the average annual intake of Coca-Cola beverages in Mexico is 225 litres per person. Mexico is thus the country in the world with the highest per capita consumption of Coca-Cola beverages, surpassing even the United States (Coca-Cola Company, 2008).

combined effects of neo-liberal adjustment accelerated by the NAFTA[2] agreement of 1994 and a greater dependency on migrant remittances, tourism, and foreign investments as a means of generating economic development. Bordering the United States in the north, Mexico is a paradigmatic case for the study of local adaptation to global processes of modernization. In many parts of Mexico, these changes have brought increased purchasing power, but also a growing dependency on commercialized, processed foods and sugar rich soft drinks together with a simultaneous decline in the significance of traditional staples such as corn and beans (Soares 2007). It can therefore be argued that sugar has been "democratized." Once an aristocratic luxury (Mintz 1985, 1997) produced by slaves and indentured labourers for the North American and European markets, sugar has today filtered down to the lower classes in Mexican society, very often in "disguised" forms as an additive in fast food and soft drinks.

Perhaps for this reason, obesity and the related disorder diabetes are today major health concerns in Mexico. It is known as the "second fattest" country in the world, and diabetes has become a leading cause of death. Once a mark of wealth, obesity is today not exclusive to the middle and upper classes or to those with greater purchasing power. Instead it has become a sign of poverty, especially in the inner cities and in rural, indigenous communities, where being overweight is especially common in the poorest segment of the population (Fernald, Gutierrez, & Neufeld et al. 2004; Zúniga et al. 2003).

The case of Coca-Cola, as well as other sweetened soft drinks, suggests that Mexico has experienced a modernization process with an associated expansion of its market and purchasing power. More than anything else, the process of modernization seems to be driven by private enterprises in a perennial quest for new markets. Consequently, today more Mexicans than ever before have access to globalized symbols of modernity, a process of adaptation which apparently occurs alongside a simultaneous decrease in dependency on traditional means of production and consumption. However, this should not lead us to interpret Mexico's consumption of Coca-Cola as nothing more than a kind of Americanization. While Coca-Cola is often seen as a symbol of Anglo-American affinity and is thus associated with an American way of life, it may also be interpreted in more or less independent ways in different local and regional settings. This suggests that Coca-Cola does not necessarily

---

2   North American Free Trade Agreement is signed by Canada, USA and Mexico. The free trade agreement came into force January 1, 1994.

mean the same thing in different places, and its presence in a given setting is therefore not – by itself – a sign of uncomplicated integration into the modern world.

In this article I will use Coca-Cola as a case in point for an analysis of the development of a distinct, heterogeneous, and contradictory version of modernity in Mexico. The major assumption of the chapter is that in Mexico there is something more going on than a local variation on European or North American models; radically new and complex cultural patterns have developed. I will discuss this issue by addressing the following questions: What meanings and values are associated with Coca-Cola and other soft drinks? What do these meanings tell us about the process of modernization in Mexico? And to what extent can we use the case of Coca-Cola consumption as a means of understanding the processes of modernization in Mexico?

I will address these questions by contrasting two different and in many ways contrasting social activities in which Coca-Cola plays a lead role: a Coca-Cola commercial that was distributed widely in Mexican TV and cinemas in 2009-2010, and the consumption of Coca-Cola as part of local religious ceremonies in Chiapas, a state in the south of Mexico. These two examples have been selected to contrast official, corporate meanings and values with those produced among the people who suffer most from obesity and diabetes, that is, poor indigenous communities.

CONSUMING COCA-COLA

The theoretical point of departure for this investigation is found in a combination of the notion of consumption (Warde 1997) and theoretical approaches concerned with what has been called "the social life of things" (Appadurai 1986). Things and commodities, like persons, lead social lives and we must therefore treat them as though they were living substances. Value and meaning are not inherent properties of objects but rather qualities derived from the ways in which objects are consumed.

Consumption is viewed as a practice. It is more than merely the intake of foods and drinks: it is also a social activity that creates meaning, and in the case of drinking globalized sweetened soft drinks such as Coca-Cola it can be argued that it is a collective or systematic mode of activity (Harvey 1996: 135). We should not attempt to read consumption as an individual activity separated from the institutional and social contexts in which it is practiced. It has of course been argued that in "late modernity" the locus of meaning is no longer grounded in loyalty to institutions (the family, the church) or structures (working class culture), but in the individual as a primary agent of meaning. This does not mean that social membership and collective meaning do no longer exist. It has been observed that, in the field of consumption, "it is comforting to know appropriate ways to act, [and] to have aesthetic judgments affirmed by like-minded people" (Warde 1997: 183), and due to its status as a global brand, it can be added that Coca-Cola is perhaps more firmly socially embedded than most other items of consumption – an argument sustained by the company's ubiquitous lifestyle advertisements representing a commercial equation of social membership and collective taste (Warde 1997: 184).

The case of Coca-Cola here becomes a problematic or complicated object of enquiry. This is not just an ordinary soft drink. It is a meta-symbol or a meta-commodity, which operates "through a powerful expressive and emotive foundation" (Miller 2005: 55). Most of all it has come to stand for Americanization, capitalism, or cultural imperialism. In analyzing the consumption of Coke as a meaning making activity, it is thus tempting to highlight the systematic factors whereby the company takes discursive and ideological control:

> Most of the literature on the company [the Coca-Cola company], irrespective of whether it is enthusiastically in favour or constructed as a diatribe against the drink, acts to affirm the assumption that the significance of the drink is best approached through knowledge of company strategy. (Miller 2005: 56)

It is indeed tempting to analyze the product's consumption as simply reproducing the official strategy of the company. Moreover, since Coca-Cola is often associated with an American way of life, the growing intake of this substance in Mexico is likely to be viewed as a desire to ape the country's perceived superiors to the north. According to this theory, taste is hierarchically ordered, and many people are eager to imitate the taste of those who are perceived as belonging to a superior level. I agree that consumption is a game of distinction (Bourdieu 1984; Gronow 1997), and that taste plays a role in defining identities, communities, and cultural differences. But it is also important to consider the local consumption cultures that often emerge, in which some of the dominant meanings and significations are rejected, contested, or simply loaded with added meanings that do not emanate from the official discourses and values.

Sidney W. Mintz has provided an illuminating overview of how colonialism transformed high-status sugar produced by slaves and forced labour into a common place staple consumed by all sectors of society (Mintz 1985). He describes how this luxury product was gradually introduced as a daily staple among working class families in Britain throughout the 19th century. But the process was not simply one of pure emulation in which the lower classes reproduced the behaviour of the upper classes. As he has emphasized in a later publication, because "there cannot be a single system of meaning for a class-divided society," the "structure of meaning" in the subsidiary, outer sectors is not "coterminous with the metropolitan heartland" (Mintz 1997: 102).

Mintz distinguishes between two different and contradictory processes to understand the ways in which sugar was transformed into a common place staple; he calls these processes intensification and extensification (1985: 122). Intensification involves continuity, referring to a process of emulation whereby sugar retains the meanings already established as consumers hark back to older usage. In contrast, extensification points our attention to the new ways of using sugar that are developed when the product is introduced to new consumers.

I will elaborate on this distinction below by asking how local consumers in the small indigenous community of San Juan de Chamula incorporate Coca-Cola into their everyday lives. This incorporation involves both intensification and the extensification of already established meanings, which are here understood as those made explicit and public through the distribution of advertisements and other means of communication controlled by the Coca-Cola Company. While intensification involves fidelity to such meanings, extensification is a process of detachment whereby older meanings are replaced by new meanings specific to the local context. It is important to point out here that although we are talking about two contradictory processes, both types of meaning will be simultaneously present in any act of consumption.

ESTÁS AQUÍ PARA SER FELIZ

The title of this section can be translated as "you are here to be happy"; it was the principal slogan of a commercial campaign that the Coca-Cola Company launched throughout the Spanish-speaking world in 2009-10. Together with another of the campaign's slogans, "destapa la felicidad" ("open happiness"), the message is clear: happiness is in the bottle and you are here to drink it.

The first slogan was also the title of a short commercial that was screened on Mexican television and in cinemas throughout 2009-10. Access to the film was also possible on Coca-Cola's Mexican homepage.[3] In the Mexican version, the commercial is a 94-second movie about a 102-year-old man named Josep Mascaró and his meeting with the mother of a newborn baby (the mother's name is Aitana Martínez Atrás). A text at the beginning of the advert tells us that the story is real,[4] and that the background for this encounter is the global economic crisis that started at the beginning of 2009, which affected many people in Mexico. There is no explicit intertextual reference to this crisis, but the wording suggests that the Coca-Cola Company as well as the old man are apparently concerned about it. At the beginning of the film, the Coca-Cola Company expresses this concern in a short meta-textual introduction:

In these difficult times, we reunite the oldest man with the youngest baby.[5]

The old man then takes on this concern by attempting to reassure Aitana, the mother of the newborn baby, that she should not worry too much:

You might be wondering why I came to know you today. Well, many will tell you that it is a bad idea to come here in the present times, that there is a crisis, that you can't make it. This will make you stronger. I have lived through worse times than these, and at the end of the day the only things you remember are the good things.[6]

Interestingly, although the wording and the use of the second person singular convey the idea of a conversation between the two characters (though Aitana Martínez is silent), Josep Mascaró is not simply acting as the protagonist of

---

3   The commercial is no longer on Coca-Cola Mexico's home-page. The film was originally produced and distributed in Spain. The Mexican version differs slightly from the original version; most importantly, some of the subtitles had been removed, among them geographical names referring to Spanish locations. The Spanish version can be accessed on Youtube: http://www.youtube.com/watch?v=bwHokw9ACQo. Accessed on October 15, 2011.
4   Translated from the Spanish: "Esta historia es real."
5   Translated from the Spanish: "En estos tiempos dificiles, reunimos al hombre más viejo con el bebe más joven."
6   Translated from the Spanish: "Te preguntarás cuál es la razón por venir a conocerte hoy. Es que muchos te dirán que a quién se le ocurre llegar en los tiempos que corren, que hay crisis, que no se puede. Esto te hará fuerte. Yo viví en momentos peores que este y al final de lo único que te vas a acordar es de las cosas buenas."

the commercial; he is simultaneously serving as its narrator, talking to the audience. There is in fact no dialogue in the film; the voice of the narrator-protagonist was probably recorded after the actual shooting of the film.[7] This throws doubt over the identity of the old man and the young mother. Is Josep Mascaró a character in the film talking to, and counseling, the young mother, or is he actually representing the Coca-Cola Company and thus addressing the perceived concerns of the Mexican audience? And, if this second interpretation has any validity, is the mother then a representation of this Mexican audience?

It is needless to say here that the film shows us more than an intergenerational encounter; it is also a meeting between a responsible, experienced person gifted with wisdom and knowledge, and a mother about to take on her shoulders the responsibility of creating and educating a new citizen (read: consumer).The old man does not reveal a preceptive attitude, attempting to tell the mother what is right and wrong. As the incarnation of many of the core values that the Coca-Cola Company apparently wishes to be associated with, he makes his point through his good example. Aside from representing wisdom and experience, the old man is also remarkably fit. At the age of 102 he dances, rides a bicycle, and is concerned with the well-being of his fellow citizens. In short, he is living a healthy lifestyle, unusually for a person of his age.

In a climate of concern about increasing consumption of soft drinks, and its possible causal relationship with the dramatic increase in modern lifestyle diseases, it has become necessary for the Coca-Cola company to address this issue. Take for example this statement from the Chief Creative Officer of the company:

> Our Achilles heel is the discussion about obesity. It's gone from a small, manageable U.S. issue to a huge global issue. It dilutes our marketing and works against it. It's a huge, huge issue. (Lee, April 23 2007).

What does the term "crisis" really refer to? Is it a reminder of the global economic crisis that began in 2009 with the financial problems in the United States and other parts of the developed world? We all know that in the begin-

---

7   There are reasons to suspect that the spoken voice is not his. After the release of the commercial Josép Mascaró acquired "celebrity status" for some time. Numerous interviews were conducted and it appears that he is only able to communicate in Mallorquín, the original dialect of the island of Mallorca. The language of the protagonist-narrator in the film is Spanish.

ning of the 2010s this is an issue of growing concern among many people in the world, including sectors of the Mexican population. But if we take a closer look at the solutions or remedies that Josep Mascaró, the protagonist-narrator of the film, suggests, there are reasons to argue that the underlying presuppositions are far more complex:

> I have lived through worse times than these, and at the end the only things you remember are the good things. Don't occupy yourself with meaningless things, they are plenty, but go searching for what makes you happy. Time passes very quickly. I've lived 102 years, and I can assure you that the only thing you won't like about life is that it will seem too short.[8]

The solution to these difficult times is not to be found in responsible economic policy, but in remembering the good things, and in searching for what makes you happy. He does not himself explicitly explain any possible sources of this happiness, but the advice "haz deporte" ("go in for sports") appears twice in large text at the bottom of the screen. Moreover, the old man himself embodies this advice through his physical activities. His dancing and bicycling serve as a visual explanation: happiness is associated with an active and healthy lifestyle, and Coca-Cola is a natural and integrated part of such a life.

On the homepage of Coca-Cola Mexico, the focus on a healthy lifestyle is accentuated in the stated goals of the company:

> Our goal: to promote active and healthy lifestyles. We believe that complete wellness is a combination of an active and healthy life, healthy coexistence, and a positive attitude. We offer people information and activities so they can fully develop. In Coca-Cola we promote active and healthy lifestyles among youth, kids, and adults. Our goal is to elevate the numbers of people practicing physical activity and doing exercise in the Mexican population, to battle sedentariness. That is why we sponsor and promote several sport programmes. To achieve equi-

---

8   Translated from the Spanish: "Yo viví en momentos peores que este y al final de lo único que te vas a acordar es de las cosas buenas. No te entretengas en tonterías que las hay y vete a buscar lo que te haga feliz. Que el tiempo corre muy de prisa. He vivido 102 años y te aseguro que lo único que no te va a gustar de la vida es que te va parecer demasiado corta."

librium between mind, body, and spirit, we support sports, healthy food habits, and a positive attitude.[9]

As part of its Corporate Social Responsibility Strategy, Coca-Cola has recently launched a new campaign titled "living positively"[10], which among many other initiatives includes investment in and the promotion of sports and other forms of physical activity in Mexican public schools.

Josep Mascaró therefore embodies the core values of Coca-Cola Company; he appears to be a person who, in virtue of his acquired wisdom, experience, and healthy lifestyle, represents most of the virtues that can address and possibly contribute a solution to the company's Achilles heel.

Finally, although Josep Mascoró is undoubtedly an expert in the art of living and in the possession of remarkable individual self-control, he is certainly not selfish. He has travelled all the way to the big city to enlighten the young mother and her newborn baby with his wisdom. The resulting encounter is an intergenerational unification that symbolizes a collective community of responsible, active, healthy, and happy consumers. The fact that the commercial was widely distributed in Mexican society through TV and cinema advertisements, as well as on Coca-Cola's webpage, underscores the commercialist function as a generator of a *sensus communitis* of happy and healthy drinkers of Coca-Cola.

The advertisement is thus also a paradigmatic illustration of Nestor Garcia Canclini's observation that in the beginning of the 21st century we are witnessing a shift from the citizen as a representative of public opinion to the consumer, who is on a quest to enjoy life (Canclini 2001: 24). But the old man's happiness is not portrayed as irresponsible. For him there is no opposition between pleasure and good. He is an incarnation of a new middle-class ethic that has replaced the morality of duty with a principle of fun

---

9   Translated from Spanish: "Nuestra Meta: Promover estilos de vida activos y saludables. Creemos que el bienestar integral es una combinación de una vida activa y saludable, la sana convivencia y una actitud positiva. Ofrecemos a las personas información y actividades para que logren desarrollarse plenamente. En Coca-Cola promovemos estilos de vida activos y saludables entre jóvenes, niños y adultos. Nuestro objetivo es elevar las cifras de la práctica de actividad física y el ejercicio entre los mexicanos para combatir el sedentarismo; por eso, patrocinamos y promovemos diversos programas deportivos. Para lograr un equilibrio entre mente, cuerpo y espíritu, fomentamos el deporte, la sana alimentación y una actitud positiva." (http://sustentabilidadcoca-cola.com.mx/estilo.html, accessed on October 21, 2011)

10   Translated from the Spanish: "viviendo positivamente."

and happiness, emphasized in the title of the commercial. But it is a reflective happiness, which in many ways differs from previous Coca-Cola commercials that focus on urban youth having spontaneous, oblivious fun. The old man consequently seems fit for tackling the challenges of late modernity, including the risks associated with the intake of unhealthy foods and drinks.

It has been said more than once that modernity "is constituted in and through reflexively applied knowledge" (Giddens 1990: 39), and that the medium of this reflexivity is the individual human being enlightened by expert systems and other sources of knowledge that serve to achieve the minimization of insecurity (Lash 1994: 116). In his theory of structuration, which was developed as far back as the early 1980s, Anthony Giddens argued that the "reflexive monitoring of action" is a chronic feature of human activity (1984), and thus not specifically connected with modernity. What is new, however, is the call for self-realization and self-control, which is closely related to the individualization of society. The old man in the Coca-Cola commercial without any doubt has this capacity, and he is therefore able to take responsibility for his own life. The question is, however, whether such a reflexively constituted modernity can be seen as a reliable depiction of all parts of contemporary Mexico. The unprecedented rise in diabetes and obesity, referred to above, suggests that the nation-wide consumption of soft drinks and other low-nu-

Coca-Cola branded plastic tables and local residents at the central square of San Juan de Chamula.

trient goods is not a pure intensification of the image of the responsible consumer. In support of this argument, I would like to explore a more implicit and localized consumption practice in the southern state of Chiapas.

CONSUMING COCA-COLA IN CHAMULA

The indigenous population of the small town of San Juan de Chamula, Chiapas, may never appear on a Coca-Cola television commercial, but the inhabitants nevertheless form part of the globalized Coca-Cola culture. As mentioned above, the goal of the Coca-Cola Company has for many years been to secure easy availability in even the remotest villages. Chamula is no exception. The Chamulan devotion to this and other soft drinks will come as a surprise to most people visiting this Tzotzil municipality, which is situated about 10 kilometres from San Cristóbal de Las Casas. It is a devotion that is cultivated hand in hand with a strong indigenous conservatism that rejects most other things from the outside world.

In front of me, I have placed two postcards that were bought outside the colonial church of San Juan Bautista in Chamula, the only church in this small indigenous town. They both show a young couple carrying out a religious ritual in which they sacrifice a chicken. The postcards help revive my memories of the powerful and peculiar syncretic religious rituals that are practiced by members of this community. The room in which the photos were taken appears to be the inside of the church, though I am unable to verify this.

The interior of the church of Chamula differs from 'normal' Catholic churches in Mexico and other parts of Latin America. On entering the church one is immediately surrounded by the smell of copal incense and the light and heat of thousands of candles placed around the floor and on tables. Most importantly, the usual rows of pews have been removed. Instead, pine needles cover the floor on which the congregation sits. Along the laterals of the nave a great number of saints' shrines are stacked, and the altar at the far end of the cathedral displays a statue of Juan Bautista (John the Baptist). During the day, individuals seeking to be cured of their ailments are congregated in front of the saints and groups of three to five villagers chant in small circles. In the centre of each circle are 30-100 candles, eggs, a live sacrificial chicken, and two or three bottles of Coca-Cola.[11] This carbonated soft drink is considered

---

[11] In the vast majority of these rituals Coca-Cola is used, but some individuals also bring Pepsi or another soft drink.

sacred and consumed –often together with a fermented corn mash called *posh* – during the rituals to make the individual who is to be cured burp. Within Chamulan syncretism Coke is believed to have curative properties, and burping is considered a way in which individuals can purify themselves by expelling evil spirits.

On arriving in this small indigenous community one is astonished by the ubiquity of Coca-Cola (and some Pepsi) signs. The town is plastered with advertisements, stickers, and glass bottles of Coke (and to a lesser extent of other fizzy drinks). Along the roads and in the central square of the town are dozens of village stores that all sell either Pepsi or Coca-Cola.[12] Outside of every shop there are always groups of villagers sitting around Coca-Cola branded plastic tables sipping Cokes.

According to some reports Coca-Cola is a booming business in this poor indigenous municipality in Chiapas, a state known to have the highest rates of malnutrition and Coke consumption in Mexico (Bell 2009). The town of Chamula is the political and commercial centre of the San Juan de Chamula municipality. Apart from the Coca-Cola shops and the cathedral, the central square is also the location of the bus station, the seat of the Mayor's office, and the office of the Institutional Revolutionary Party (Partido Revolucionario Institucional, PRI). The central square, with its tangible symbols of religious, commercial, and political power, reminds the townspeople of how closely these authorities are intertwined. Chamula is known for its historical and present leanings towards the Institutional Revolutionary Party (Fonseca 2004), as well as for its own internal power relations. According to Christine Kovic, many villagers support the PRI for material benefits and to limit outside intervention in local affairs (Kovics 2005: 2).

The town is characterized by a rigid centralism and a historically grounded "community autonomy," which has been defended by a small number of wealthy caciques with close relations to the PRI. Despite a formal municipal democracy, the real political and economic power is therefore in the hands of these caciques, who are wealthy land owners or business runners. Some of the most powerful caciques have for many years been in control of the sale of soft drinks (Díaz-Cayeros & Magaloni 2003: 257). According to many reports, they also control much of the political life of Chamula, and they maintain close relations with the City Mayor, who is always a member of the PRI. Perhaps for this reason, Coke also plays a role in negotiations with

12   Each store usually only sells one brands.

local authorities. Requests for permissions, for example to build or enlarge a house, must be accompanied by Coke offerings (Johnson 2004). In Chamula, Coca-Cola has thus become more than just a soft drink. It is an integral part of the everyday social, religious, and political life of the municipality. Coca-Cola has thus been successful in connecting itself not only to the economy, but also to the powerful elites who have political, cultural, and religious control over the population (Borden 2004a).

The Coca-Cola Company has achieved its goal of reaching remote communities as regards Chamula. Introduced to the community about 50 years ago, the soft drink is today an easily accessed commodity for most villagers. Moreover, it has been incorporated into both religious and political life has thus been endowed with meanings and usages that differ from those sanctioned by the company. The Company's narrative portrays the drink as part of an active and healthy lifestyle and as the locus of a *sensus communitis* inhabited by autonomous yet responsible citizens, who have acquired the wisdom and the knowledge necessary to face the risks and insecurities of the modern world.

It is important here to emphasize the socio-economic situation in Chamula. The municipality is ranked as one of the poorest in Mexico, and it has been characterized as one of the socially most vulnerable municipalities in the state of Chiapas, which has the highest level of marginalization in the country (Soares 2007). Only half of the dwellings have access to clean drinking water, only 62% of the population speaks Spanish, and infant mortality rates are extremely high (Diaz-Cayeros 2003: 256-58). Based on her investigations in Pozuelas, a small community in the municipality of Chamula, Soares also describes the educational system as deficient. The same goes for the health service; the population often depends on traditional medicine (Soares 2007: 33).

MODERNITY WITH DEFICIENT MODERNIZATION

Renato Ortiz has argued that, unlike Europe, Latin America sees modernity as a project, something to be achieved in the future. Modernism has therefore first and foremost existed as a discursive phenomenon or as an array of narratives about the future, without ever corresponding to a social reality (Ortiz 2000: 254). Some observers detect a "broken" modernity in contemporary Latin America, one that is the result of a particular process of modernization in which the private sector has played the primary role (Canclini 2001). The outcome of these changes is reflected in widespread and diversified development, based on the use of more advanced technologies (Ortiz 2000: 257). In the wake of this development there has been an increase in the markets for cultural goods, particularly communication technologies such as television.

In Mexico, television is today available everywhere in the country, providing the great majority with access to telenovelas, commercials, and other sources of audiovisual information. Ortiz argues that this development completely transformed popular culture in Latin America, replacing the old loci of communities (the village, the region) with new patterns of sociability that cut across the old identities, which are taken for granted. With the decline in the importance of old institutions, there has been a rise in participation in transnational and deterritorialized communities of consumers (Canclini 2001: 24). Corporate businesses such as Coca-Cola and Televisa[13] have been primary agents in this attainment of globalized information and consumption opportunities, and with the neoliberal tribute to deregulation and privatization modernity now appears "to the majority only as [an object] of consumption, and for many as little more than a show to be watched" (Canclini 2001: 26). A notorious characteristic of contemporary Mexico is thus the development of a contradictory modernity where citizenship is not exercised fully. This tendency is underscored by deficient schooling systems, which have been underfunded as part of the neoliberal orthodoxy. Schools, Ortiz argues, therefore fail to compete with the cultural industries in influencing the young (2000: 257-58). In his analysis of the nutritional consequences of the introduction and proliferation of "hybrid cuisines" in Mexico, Jeffrey M. Pilcher maintains that this is part of the reason why traditional cooking has been devalued, giving rise to new eating and drinking patterns in which fast food and soft drinks have become fashionable:

> They [Mexican politicians] conceded to food manufacturers the educational power of the mass media, allowing massive advertising campaigns for soft drinks and snack candies, with a 'small print' advice to eat fresh fruits and vegetables included as the only concessions to public health. (Pilcher 2005: 245)

Underfunded schooling and corporate nutritional disinformation must be seen within the context of the neo-liberal changes that were introduced after the economic crisis of the mid-1980s. Pilcher mentions the elimination at the end

---

13   Grupo Televisa was founded in 1955 and is a large Mexican mass media company broadcasting throughout Latin america and the United States.

of the 1990s of the subsidy programmes that used to support the national production of daily staples such as corn and beans (2005: 235). Consequent rising prices have contributed to changing eating and drinking patterns with more poor families relying on fast food, cheap wheat pasta, and other calorie- and sugar-dense but nutrient-poor foods. In their study of what they call the "Coca-colonization of diets in Yucatan," Leatherman and Goodman come to a similar conclusion, although they pay attention to how other aspects of the neo-liberal paradigm such as increased tourism and migration have resulted in a commoditization of diets and nutrition (Leatherman & Goodman 2004). Many people, including members of indigenous communities, have acquired increased purchasing power and access to a greater variety of consumer goods, but this development has occurred at the cost of a disruption in traditional subsistence activities, including a decline in agricultural productivity.

The same tendency can be seen in Chamula, where production is today insufficient on the traditional small subsistence plots, and there is therefore a growing dependency on salary work and other sources of earnings, among them the sale of handicrafts to tourists in San Cristóbal de las Casas (Soares 2007: 33). The result is a movement away from traditional diets, a decline in dietary diversity, and an increase in the intake of low-nutrient snack foods and sweetened soft drinks. Leatherman and Goodman describe this as a "dou-ble-edged sword of malnutrition, where childhood malnutrition is replaced by adult obesity later in life" (2005: 834). This conclusion is underscored by various health studies conducted in Mexico, which reveal a combined geo-graphical and demographical polarization with malnutrition most prevalent among indigenous minorities in the south (Zúnega et al. 2003).

BIBLIOGRAPY

Appadurai, A. (1986). *The Social life of Things. Commodities in Cultural Perspective.* Cambridge: Cambridge University Press.

Beck, U. (1992). *Risk Society. Towards a New Modernity.* London: Sage Publications.

Bell, B. (2006, October 6). Cola wars in Mexico. *In These Times.* Retrieved from http://inthese-times.com/article/2840/cola_wars_in_mexico

Borden, T. (2004a, April 14). In Chiapas, Cola is king. *Atlanta-Journal Constitution.* Retrieved from http://www.prolades.com/news/Traditional%20healers%20put%20Coke%20to%20the%20test.htm

Borden, T. (2004b, April 14). Traditional healers put Coke to the test. *Atlanta-Journal Consti-tution.* Retrieved from http://www.prolades.com/news/Traditional%20healers%20put%20Coke%20to%20the%20test.htm

Bourdieu, P. (1984). *Distinction. A social Critique of the Judgment of Taste.* London: Routledge and Kegan Paul.

Diaz-Cayeros, E., & Magaloni, B. (2003). *Improving Living Conditions: The Effects of Social Transfers on Public Good Provision.* Unpublished manuscript.

Canclini, N.G. (2001). *Consumers and Citizens. Globalization and Multicultural Conflicts.* Minneapolis: University of Minneapolis Press.

Coca-Cola Company (2008). *Per Capita Consumption of Company Beverage Products.* Retrieved from http://www.thecoca-colacompany.com/ourcompany/ar/pdf/perCapitaConsumption2008. pdf

Fernald, L. C., Gutierrez, J.P., Neufeld, L. M. et al. (2004). High prevalence of obesity among the poor in Mexico. *Journal of the American Medical Association,* vol. 291, issue 21, pp. 2544-2545.

Fonseca, G.M.C. (2004). México. The colors of Chiapas. *Revista Envio,* vol. 280. Retrieved from http://www.envio.org.ni/articulo/2675

Giddens, A. (1990). *The Consequences of Modernity.* Cambridge: Polity Press.

Gledhill, J. (1999). *Getting new bearings in the labyrinth: The transformation of the Mexican State and the real Chiapas.* (Unpublished manuscipt). University of Manchester.

Gronow, J. (1997). *The Sociology of Taste.* New York: Routledge.

Harvey, P. (1996). *Hybrids of Modernity: Anthropology, the Nation State and the Universal Exhibition.* London: Routledge.

Lash, S. (1995). Reflexivity and its doubles: structure, aesthetics, community. In U. Beck, A. Giddens, & S. Lash (Eds.), *Reflexive Modernization. Politics, Tradition, Aesthetics in the Modern Social Order.* Cambridge: Polity Press.

Leatherman, T.L., & Goodman, A. (2005). Coca-colonization of diets in the Yucatan. *Social Science and Medicine,* vol. 61, pp. 833-846.

Lee, E. (2007). Quoted in S. Thompson & K. Macarthur, Obesity Fear Frenzy Grips Food Industry. Why Coke's Creative Chief Esther Lee isn't Alone in Fearing FTC Critics. *Advertising Age,* April 23, 2007. Retrieved from http://adage.com/print/116233.

Miller, D. (2005). Coca-Cola: A black sweet drink from Trinidad. In J. Watson & M. Caldwell (Eds.), *The Cultural Politics of Food and Eating.* Malden: Blackwell Publishing.

Mintz, S. (1985). *Sweetness and Power: the Place of Sugar in Modern History.* New York: Viking.

Mintz, S. (1997). Time, sugar, and sweetness. In C. Couniham & P. Van Esterik (Eds.), *Food and Culture. A Reader.* New York: Routledge.

Ortiz, R. (2000). From incomplete modernity to world modernity. *Deadalus,* vol. 129, 1, pp. 249-260.

Pendergast, M. (2000). *For God, Country and Coca-Cola: the Unauthorized History of the Great American Soft Drink and the Company That Makes it.* New York: Charles Scribner's Sons.

Rivera, J.A. et al. (2008). Consumo de bebidas para una vida saludable: recomendaciones para la población Mexicana. *Salud pública de México,* vol. 50, issue 2, pp. 172-194.

Soares, D. (2007). Acceso, abasto y control del agua en una comunidad indígena chamula en Chiapas. Un análisis a través de la perspectiva de género, ambiente y desarollo. *Región y Sociedad,* vol. 19, issue 38, pp. 25-50.

Vartanian, L.R, & Schwartz, M.B. (2007). Effects of soft drink consumption on nutrition and health: A systematic review and meta-analysis. *American Journal of Public Health,* vol. 97, issue 4, pp. 667-675.

Warde, A. (1997). *Consumption, Food & Taste.* London: Sage Publications.

Zúniga, M.C.C., Fritch, H.M., Villa, A.R., & Soto, N.G. (2003). Alta prevalencia de desnutrición en la población infantil indígena Mexicana. Encuesta nacional de nutrición 1999. *Revista Especial Salud Pública*, vol. 77, pp. 245-255.

CHAPTER V

The Sweet Tooth of Mother Earth: Sugar's Symbolic Ways Among the Highland Indians in Bolivia

By Annie Oehlerich

Sugar is one of the basic principles in the Quechua rites addressed to the feminine pre-Columbian Goddess Pachamama, or Mother Earth. It has been deeply integrated into the social life and symbolic structures of the community as part of the cosmology since the time of the Inca Empire. Sugar is part of the naturalistic humeral cold/warm food system used by the Quechua, in which the body is in balance with the natural environment. Sugar has great symbolic value: it is an interface between man and the cosmic world in a collective ritual that also connects the individual with society. These sacrificial sugar rituals to the pre-Columbian fertility Goddess are also part of a new trend in Bolivia, where even political candidates carry out sugar rituals 'in the Indian way', as part of the new national political context. This chapter describes the different symbolic values of sugar in the social life of the Bolivian Quechua peasants.

SUGAR CONSUMPTION AND SUGAR RITUALS IN BOLIVIA

Like most Latin American countries, Bolivia consumes a lot of sugar. The huge lowlands are warm and humid, and the production of sugar cane in these areas increased in 2012 by 20%: 45,3 million kg of sugar cane were produced in this year alone. The population's sugar intake is shockingly high, at around 7,5 million kg per annum. Consumption patterns are shifting as people migrate from the countryside to the cities and a sugar-filled lifestyle. Because of globalization, it is now easy to find sweet soft drinks as Coca-Cola in almost all corners of the countryside, and the intake of this and popular fast food may create health problems as diabetes. However, this article does not have its focus on the major health problems that this sugar consumption causes, but on the symbolic meaning of the sugar for the indigenous population in the highland. Sugar is the candy of the gods and is used in traditional rites addressed to Pachamama, Mother Earth. The following analysis has been written on the basis of many years' fieldwork and residence in Bolivia between 1986 and the present. According to the last housing survey conducted in Bolivia, in 2001, the majority of the 10 million people living in the country are indigenes (62%). Over 50% of the total population belong to the Quechua and Aymara groups, the largest groups in the mountains. These people have lived high in the Andes of Bolivia and Peru for centuries, since the time of the Inca Empire. The Quechua lived in extended families in small peasant villages on the mountainside; their subsistence economy meant that agrarian products such as potatoes and quinoa constituted the basic diet. This economy was supplemented by llama herding and temporary migration to the big cities. Sugar was an important part of their life, not in their daily diet but as a symbol in their cosmology, social practices, and traditional medicine with which they venerated Mother Earth and attempted to live in harmony with nature.

Today, sugar rituals are still in use, but not restricted to Bolivia's indigenous population. During election campaigns, political candidates typically take part in sacrifice rituals, creating their own ritual packages for Mother Earth and never forgetting to give a few drops of beer or *Chicha* to Mother Earth before they drink from their own glass. The rituals performed by these political candidates do not belong to any ethnic groups, but in performing indigenous rites and giving Mother Earth her candy, they demonstrate respect for and identification with ancient indigenous values. They sacrifice sugar to the pre-Columbian fertility goddess and make sugar 'the Indian way,' in a new national political context.

Sugar is thus an important ingredient in a contemporary political trend to do with Andean indigenous identity in Bolivia. The government of the indigenous president Evo Morales is promoting a cultural and democratic revolution. Their political agenda includes decolonizing society and formulating alternatives to neo-liberalism, hence their uses of idealist notions of Andean culture to promote this agenda (Postero 2007). It includes a removal of the Western values left over from the colonial era in medical, legal, and educative systems (and so on), and instead a focus on indigenous rights and popular democracy, as well as recognition of indigenous culture, values, and symbols. The sacred sugar rituals and *challa* to Mother Earth are part of Bolivia's modern political identity.

SUGAR FOR THE DEAD

The Quechua believe in life after death and have been celebrating their dead ancestors since the time of the Inca Empire. Following Spanish colonization and the introduction of the Roman Catholic Church, a syncretism ritual developed that combined both belief systems: *el dia de Todos los Santos*, the day of the deceased, is an annual event celebrated on the November 2. On this day, the favourite foods of the deceased – such as boiled potatoes, quinoa, chili, raw sugar, cake, and/or a specially constructed glazed quinoa biscuit called *k'ispiña* – are placed before the house altar. Families gather to pray together in front of the altar and then go to the cemetery together, where they remember the dead throughout the night, surrounded by bright lights and festivities. The sugar is given in order to sweeten the life beyond this one. Having spent the night at the tomb along with all the other families remembering their loved ones, they go home and eat the offerings on the family altar.

THE FOOD CATEGORIES

In order to understand the function of sugar within these religious rituals, it is necessary to understand that sugar is one part of a whole system based on the division of both food and diseases into "hot" and "cold" categories. Potatoes are hot, salt is cold, and sugar is hot; these concepts are both metaphorical and literal. The indigenous people of the Andes not only feel healthy when their bodies are in balance, with a 'normal' body temperature, but the status of their health status on this internal balance between the hot and cold. Imbalance in bodily fluids is perceived to affect the body's normal health. Body temperature rises and falls, while food has an innate nature that does not change. The classification of food and/or medications into either cold or hot categories is part of an indigenous internal symbolic language.

The indigenous humoral systems have existed for many years, and they have been blended with the medical systems of the Spanish colonialists. The humoral health theories, where foods are classified as cold or hot, in a meaningful balance system, are known throughout most of South America and have been described by many anthropologists (e.g. Fock 1982; Foster 1976; Libbet Crandon-Malamud 1991).

The Quechua in Bolivia, Peru, and Ecuador cook their food using the hot/cold system. Their daily diet is preventive, intended to counteract imbalances in the body. Temperature changes across a life span, so that children are born cold and older people die hot. Children often get heat illnesses such as fever (in Spanish fever is called *calentura*, which means "heat"), while older people suffer from arthritis, a cold disease that can be counteracted by a hot meal after waking up cold in the morning (Fock 1982). The body's equilibrium is an expression of a cosmic dualistic worldview, in which man exists between two extremes. The system works prophylactically, the balance is maintained through the daily food. Eating too many 'hot' foods like sugar will make you vulnerable to certain diseases that should be healed with 'cold' herbs, and vice versa – cold diseases are cured by hot foods or herbs that are considered to be 'hot' (Oehlerich 1992). The system appears simple but is actually very complex; cold water is 'cold,' but so is hot water. Some diseases, such as *susto*, or 'soul loss' (a Latin American illness category), are described as warm, but since they are caused by external events, they are considered more serious than an imbalance in the body. The warm magical diseases are difficult to cure and require visits to a specialist. Categorizations like these are not always the same among the various mountain villages, although the equilibrium system is the same. Treatment requires a thorough knowledge of food categories and disease classifications.

THE SWEET TOOTH OF MOTHER EARTH

The Indians' categorizations of foodstuffs are based on their religious beliefs about balance in life. The universe consists of two halves, which are held up against each other: sun and moon, male and female, day and night. This duality is reflected in the perception of good and evil – anything and everything contains both forces. The world is built upon a balanced dualism, where every individual or concept justifies and explains another's existence. The cosmic dimension is so deeply rooted in the Indians' daily lives that it affects their social behaviour patterns. Society is built around a collective value system, where a closely linked social network is developed through economic and social exchange relationships that provide assurance of social existence. This internal indigenous organization of the village weaves the families together in a pattern of services and compensations. Food is an important ingredient in a number of these reciprocal services.

The most important of these collective institutions are *Minka*, *Mita*, and *Aini*. *Minka-minga* is a form of reciprocal exchange that comes into force at sowing and harvesting. Everyone comes together voluntarily to participate in the work, all for a single family. This family provides food for the workers in return. In Quechua, *Minga* describes an individual person calling for help. *Minka* means "food," and a communal meal is mandatory repayment for the minka-work. Through the social institution of *Minka* families can ask others for a service in return for a meal. This repayment is expected (Johnson 1986).

Mita is used by the government administration to build roads and schools, among other things. Again, it works on the principle of taking turns to serve one another: each family is required to work a specified number of days a year on these communal projects. Finally, the *Aini* is a reciprocal exchange system that regulates borrowing, for anything from food to social assistance. Repayment is always made in kind. From the moment a person helps another person, a dependence relationship exists until the debt has been paid back. The roles of donor and recipient are always switching around as everybody plays both at some point. *Aini* can be interpreted as the start of social imbalance, but it also provides an opportunity to give back.

This reciprocal relationship is reflected in the attitude to the pre-Columbian Goddess Pachamama. The entire universe is perceived as one living organism, in which Mother Earth and man mutually guarantee each other's continuity. Farmers cultivate the earth, giving birth to the gods, and the cosmic universe bestows fertility. The divine powers in turn ensure human reproduction. These gods have human traits: Mother Earth and the spirits need to drink and eat, so meals are sacrificed to them.

Conceptions of health and illness among indigenous people living in the Andes are affected by their cosmology. The concept of nature is expanded and influenced by climatic factors like snow, rain, hail, and lightning. Bad weather and natural disasters are all signs that some human flaw has disturbed the balance between the cosmos and man. If the harvest fails or hail destroys the crops, it is human sin that is the cause. As such, the whole social structure rests on harmonious equilibrium, not only between individuals, but also between the gods and man. It is important to honor the supernatural in everyday life to prevent the release of their vengeful forces. This concept of harmony, in which everyone and everything is contained in a complete, living process, is broken by conflicts either on the outer or the inner level. To maintain social order, conflicts must be avoided through preventive work. The cosmic universe is omnipresent and the Indians are the focal point of the sacral forces, since they live at the centre of the world.

To placate the gods the Quechua symbolically offer meals in sacred packets with sugar and perform reconciliation rituals, thanking the gods for their protection. A reconciliation ritual can last an entire day, and it is a great social event since all community members participate.

The agrarian cycle can be divided into three great epochs: the dry season from June to August when the grain is sown and the Indians pray for a good harvest; the rainy season from August to January, when crops grow; and the cold period from February to May, when the harvest is brought in and the village makes a big collective ritual sacrifice in gratitude. Rituals often take place in accordance with the agrarian cycle or Catholic holidays such as Easter, Pentecost, Carnival, and All Saints. The most rituals occur in August, since this is the time when the mountain spirits are most hungry; it is said that the mouths are open in August. The sacred rituals are called *challas*, and it is an effective preventive action in daily life. It is also always a reciprocal social act, so that whilst good rituals bring health, luck, good business, and marriage, etc., bad rituals bring death and sickness to humans or animals. Mother Earth is just as dangerous as she is good.

Sacrificial rituals are collective, and everybody contributes something. Government officials will bring the major offerings such as a sheep. The ritual package consists of cigarettes, coca leaves, alcohol, and mineral and animal products, but its main constituent is sugar, because Mother Earth has a sweet tooth.

The Indians call these sugar offerings *MISA de la dulce*, the sweet sermon, and they take the form of sugar plates and figurines of Mother Earth made of coloured sugar. These *dulces* can be purchased in the form of candies, sweets, and animal figures, depending on the purpose. *MISA de la dulce* is an important constituent of all good ritual packages. Besides sugar figurines the sacrifice will contain dried fruits like figs, nutmegs, and *los mistérios*, which are small coloured squares symbolically stamped with images such as cars, bills, or animals, depending on the purpose. *Mistérios* are made by flour mixed with lime to make them hard; the sugar plates are printed with symbols and people in relief. The images are always related to the purpose of the package and provide a magical relationship with the divinity. For example, a white plate with a motif of a loving couple is used in sacrificial rituals for weddings, an image of a llama indicates a direct gift to Mother Earth, and a yellow sun represents a desire for fertility (Girault 1988: 271; Oehlerich 1992). The tradition of sugar packets has its origins in the Andean religion, but they may also depict Christian figures such as Jesus on the Cross or Catholic saints.

Most highland Indians in Bolivia know the significance of these sugar figures, but to carry out a sacrificial ritual they must turn to traditional healers.

Only the medicine men and women are familiar with the precise composition and execution of rituals whose key element is always the exchange of food with Mother Earth.

Sugar has thus a great symbolic value, it is an interface between man and the cosmic world, in a collective ritual that connects the individual with society and the sacred world.

CONCLUDING REMARKS

Sugar's symbolic importance is part of the traditional highland culture of the Andes, with deep roots in the area's history. Sugar cane came to Bolivia from the large sugar plantations in Brazil after the Spanish conquest of America, but the traditional healers of the Andes, known as the *Kallawayas* or *Yatiris*, have performed the *Ch'alla*, the Andean ritual to Mother Earth, for over 500 years. It has always been characterized by the burial of coca leaves, corn flour, cigarettes, and sweet plants to nourish and honor Mother Earth.

The *Ch'alla* and the symbolic use of sugar have played significant roles in the political development of indigenous identity in the Bolivian Andes. It has never been more modern than it is now. In the Indian universe, sugar has a high status as the food of Gods. Recognising and understanding the cultural roles of foodstuffs, like that of sugar in Andean cosmology, reminds us that food categories can be understood from multiple angles.

BIBLIOGRAPHY

Crandon-Malamud, L. (1991). *From the Fat of Our Souls*. Berkeley: University of California Press.

Fock, N. (1982). *Mellem det varme og det kolde*. Jordens Folk, vol. 17, issue 4, pp. 164-173.

Foster, G. (1978). Hippocrates' Latin American legacy: "Hot" and "cold" in contemporary folk medicine. *Colloquia in Anthropology*, vol. 2,, pp. 3-19.

Foster, G. (1976). Disease etiologies in non-Western medical systems. *American Anthropologist*, vol. 78, pp. 773-782

Girault, L. (1988). Kallawaya: Curanderos. *Itinerantes de los Andes*.

Johnson, M. (1986). Food and culture among Bolivian aymara: Symbolic expressions of social relations. *Uppsala Studies in Cultural Anthropology*.

Oehlerich, A. (1992). Pachamama, protegeme, sygdom og behandlingsstrategier i andes. (Unpublished Master's thesis). Copenhagen: University of Copenhagen.

Postero, N. (2007). Andean utopias in Evo Morales's Bolivia. *Latin American and Caribbean Ethnic Studies*, vol. 2, issue 1, pp. 1-28.

CHAPTER VI

Production Methods and Quality of Sugar Cane in Latin America

By Gitte K. Bjørn and Ulla Kidmose

In 2010, approximately 154 million tons of sugar was produced worldwide, with approximately 80% coming from sugar cane and the remainder from sugar beets. Sugar cane production is a big business in many Latin American countries. However, there are many challenges with respect to sugar cane production that can significantly affect the sugar yield. These challenges will be reviewed in this chapter.

SUGAR CANE AND SUGAR

Sugar cane is a tall perennial grass of the genus *Saccharum*. It has stout, jointed, fibrous stalks that are rich in sugar, and grows to between two and six metres tall (Fig. 1). All sugar cane species interbreed, and the major commercial cultivars are complex hybrids. Sugar cane cultivation requires a tropical or temperate climate, with a minimum of 60 centimetres of annual moisture. Sugar cane is a C4 plant,[1] and is one of the most efficient crops in utilizing solar energy.

Sucrose is the most abundant sugar found in sugar cane. It is a disaccharide that consists of one molecule of glucose and one molecule of fructose. In sucrose, glucose and fructose are bound together with a β-1,4-glucosidic

---

[1]   C4 plants are plants that create four carbon (C4) molecules when performing photosynthesis in contrast to common plants that create molecules with three carbons (known as C3 plants).

Figure 1. A sugar cane field (Photo: Per Bendix Jeppesen, Aarhus University).

bound. In general sucrose is called sugar, because table sugar is sucrose. In sugar cane, the content of sucrose can be up to 20% of the dry weight in the mature internodes (Halford et al. 2011).

SUGAR CANE PRODUCTION

Brazil is the world's largest producer of sugar cane. Ninety per cent of Brazil's sugar is made in the south-central region and the remainder is produced in the northeast. The timing of the rainy period and the humidity balance are important for the total yield. In 2010, the rainy period started before the harvesting season, which enhanced the development of the plants. In 2009, excess rain between April and November halved the output of the mills, because high humidity reduces the sucrose content in the sugar cane significantly. The Brazilian public crop forecasting agency Conab expected Brazilian mills to produce about 37 million tons of sugar in 2010, and 33.1 million tons in 2009 (Bloomberg 2010). In 2010, Brazilian mills produced record quantities of sugar and ethanol from sugar cane; the proportions of ethanol and sugar produced were 54.6% and 45.4% respectively. The current trend shows that Brazil is exporting more and more sugar. Table 1 lists the top ten sugar cane producers in 2008 (FAOSTAT 2010); many Latin Americans make the list, including Brazil, Mexico, Colombia, and Argentina.

Country	Production (Tons)*
Brazil	645,300,182
India	348,187,900
People's Republic of China	124,917,502
Thailand	73,501,610
Pakistan	63,929,000
Mexico	51,106,900
Colombia	38,500,000
Australia	33,973,000
Argentina	29,950,600
United States of America	27,603,000
World	1,736,271,147

Table 1. The top ten sugar cane producers in 2008 (FAOSTAT, 2010).
*American measurement. Source: FAOSTAT, Food and Agriculture Organization of the United Nations, 2010, http://faostat.fao.org/site/567

VARIETIES OF SUGAR CANE

Sugar cane is an ancient crop with a complex genetic history. Until the 20th century, sugar cane industries throughout the world relied on noble canes (*Saccharum officinarum* L.) for sugar production. However, since the early 20th century most of the production world-wide has been derived from polyploid, aneuploid interspecific hybrids of two or more basic *Saccharum* species. Sucrose yield in sugar cane is a product of cane yield and sucrose content of the cane (Lingle et al. 2010). Sugar cane varieties differ significantly in their ability to accumulate sucrose, which result in differences in sucrose yield between different varieties (Halford et al. 2011). According to Jackson (2005), sugar yield has increased from approximately 4 tons/hectare to approximately 13 tons/hectare from historical to recent sugar cane varieties in the Herbert region of Australia. It is clear from this that the choice of variety has a high impact on sugar yield.

To improve the efficiency of the Brazilian industry, new sugar cane varieties with higher yields are continuously being developed and tested. An ideal sugar cane variety should be well adapted to local variations in climate, soil type, and cutting system (manual or mechanized) or ratooning[2]. It should be

---

2   Ratoon means a shoot sprouting from a plant base.

resistant to pests, diseases, and water stress and it should have high accumulation of sucrose in the storage tissue (Galvão, Formaggio, & Tisot 2004).

In 2007, the Cane Technology Centre (CTC), a private company in the state of Sao Paulo, obtained approval from the Brazilian authorities for field trials of three varieties of genetically modified sugar cane. According to the organization, these GM plants have been modified to exhibit sucrose levels 15% higher than those of ordinary sugar cane – for now, only under laboratory conditions. However, if the field trials are successful, the company may bring these plants to the market in the future (GMO Compass 2007). The development of CTC's high-sucrose GM plants builds on the success of the Brazilian Sugar Cane EST Genome Project (SUCEST). This project was carried out by several Brazilian universities between 1998 and 2003, and its results were used to establish a database that integrated genome sequences for this crop. Subsequently CTC, the Lucelia Central Alcohol Distillery, and various universities analyzed more than 2,000 sugar cane genes. Researchers found and patented 200 target genes related to the accumulation of sucrose in the plant. In 2007, the federal government announced plans to fund biotechnological research, including the development of a new strain of sugar cane that is resistant to drought. By developing canes with this characteristic, Brazil may be able to expand crops into areas that are substantially drier than the south-central region of Brazil.

In 2010 Bayer CropScience and CTC entered into a broad cooperation on the research and development of biotech sugar cane varieties. The main goal is to combine the expertise of both partners to develop varieties with higher sugar content. The new biotech varieties are expected to produce up to 40% more sugar than is possible at present (Bayer CropScience, 2010). A new variety with 25% increased yield is expected to be commercially available in Brazil by 2020 (GMO Compass 2007).

NUTRIENT SUPPLY DURING CULTIVATION

As a giant crop that produces a huge quantity of biomass, sugar cane generally demands a high amount of nutrient elements. A large number of research experiments have clearly demonstrated that for the production of higher cane and sugar yields on a sustainable basis, application of adequate amounts of fertilizer, that is nitrogen (N), phosphorus (P), and potassium (K), is essential. The fertilizer recommendations for sugar cane in different countries are given in Table 2 (Netafim 2011).

Country	Crop	Nutrients (kg/ha)			Remarks
		N	P₂O₅	K₂O	
Brazil:					
North East	Plant cane	60-80	80-180	30-120	N – 2/3 side-
	Ratoon	60-80	20-100	40-140	dressed
South East	Plant cane	50-90	50-110	20-120	P & K according
	Ratoon	50-90	25-50	10-80	to soil analysis
Central West	Plant cane	30-40	30-120	30-120	
	Ratoon	40-60	15-60	20-90	
South	Plant cane	40-100	0-120	30-120	
	Ratoon	20-40	20-60	0-60	
Colombia	Plant cane	50-70	50-100	60-150	N – side-dressed
	Ratoon	50-100	60-120	60-150	according to leaf analysis. P & K rates depending upon soil analysis
Costa Rica	Plant cane	80-200	60-200	80-200	
	Ratoon	100-250	50-200	80-250	
Cuba	Plant cane	0	0-50	0-120	P & K rates de-
	Ratoon	35-150	0-50	0-150	pending upon soil analysis and yield level

Table 2. Recommended nutrient doses in different countries (After Netafim,
www.sugarcanecrops.com/agronomic_practices/fertigation/28.htm.)

OPTIMAL TIMES FOR FERTILIZATION

As shown in Figure 2, nutrient accumulation pattern as a function of crop ontogeny has to be taken in to account for the timing of fertilizer application.

The nitrogen requirement of sugar cane is greatest during the tillering phase (Fig. 1). This is required for adequate tiller production and canopy development. Tillering in field grown sugar cane starts around 40 days after planting. Adequate N supply should be made available to the crop in the soil from the start of the tillering phase. Furthermore, the crop's requirement for N is

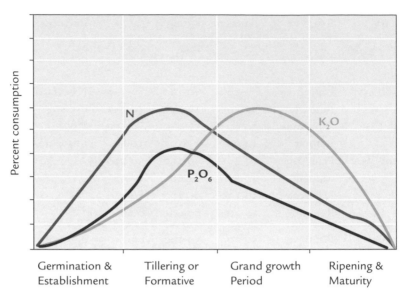

Figure 2. Relative requirement of NPK at different crop growth stages of sugar cane (Bachchhav 2005).

higher early in the grand growth period than it is later in the grand growth period and in the ripening and maturity periods (Fig. 2).

The annual application of nitrogen fertilizer for Brazilian sugar cane is around 50 kg N/ha[-1]. A field study showed the combined effect of nitrogen application and irrigation on the cane yield as well on the sugar yield and content (Wiedenfeld 1995). Both juice purity and sugar yield decreased significantly with decreasing levels of irrigation. However, the effect of nitrogen application on cane yield and its quality interacted with irrigation level and crop year. The nitrogen application did not affect the sugar yield or juice purity in the plant cane, but it did have a pronounced effect on sugar yield and juice purity in both first and second ratoon (Wiedenfeld 1995).

If N-fertilizer application could be reduced by one half due to biological nitrogen fixation (BNF), a fixation of the atmospheric nitrogen in association with the bacterium *Glucoacetobacter diazotrophicus* that some sugar cane varieties are capable of, producers could save an estimated US$ 62.5 millon/y[-1]. It is well known that the beneficial interactions between plants and bacteria are genotype- and site-specific. Most of the work on BNF in the sugar cane rhizophere has been conducted in Brazil. Brazilian sugar cane varieties can obtain up to 70% of their nitrogen requirement from BNF, and this contribution is related to Brazilian breeding and selection processes (de Oliveira et al. 2006).

Leaching of nitrogen is very prevalent as in most sugar cane areas application rates are high, rainfall or irrigation are abundant, and nitrogen use recovery is low. Studies on nitrogen leaching from sugar cane crops in Brazil have been limited – possibly because nitrogen applications here are low, as mentioned earlier, since much of the nitrogen in Brazilian sugar cane is derived from BNF (Hartemink 2008).

Phosphorus need is highest during the formative phase of the sugar cane crop (Fig. 2). Thus, the optimum time for P application is during the initial stages of crop growth. Sufficient P must be made available in the soil during the formative phase for absorption by the crop.

Potassium applications are usually made along with N applications. This is due to the crop's optimal utilization of N in the presence of K. However, late application of K at around six months has also been found to improve sugar recovery.

The sugar cane plant can be harvested several times annually. After each harvest, new stalks (ratoons) are developed. Sugar cane is harvested by hand or mechanically.

MANUAL HARVESTING

Hand harvesting accounts for more than half of all sugar cane production and is still dominant in many developing countries in Central and South Africa and Central and South America. However, in some countries such as Brazil the areas that are manually harvested decreased drastically between 2002 and 2009 (www.dfid.gov.uk). The sugar cane plant consists of about 75% net cane (stalks) from which the juice is extracted and the sugar crystallized. The other 25% of the plant consists of leafy material, including tops, from which little or no sugar is produced. This leafy material is called trash. Burning sugar cane before harvest removes between one-half and two-thirds of this material. Before manual harvesting, the field is set on fire to facilitate more efficient harvest and transport. Besides burning the dry leaves, it also kills any venomous snakes and other wildlife that has managed to survive in the sugar cane fields. Harvesters then cut the cane just above ground level using cane knives or machetes.

BURNED AND UNBURNED HARVEST SYSTEMS

Sugar cane cropping is expanding in Brazil. The majority of the production of this crop is still dependent on the activity of small farmers in the Rio de

Janeiro State. Traditional sugar cane management is based on pre-harvest burning, but this causes a loss of organic matter and volatile nutrients. The burning also leads to emissions of greenhouse gases (GHGs) (e.g. CO_2, CH_4, and N_2O) besides the release of charcoal (BC) particles into the atmosphere. Some countries, including Brazil, have introduced legislation against the burning of cane fields, because of economic and environmental concerns (Galdos et al. 2010). Around 10-15 Mg ha^{-1} per year (trash and flag leaves) is to the soil as a consequence of not burning (Graham, Hayes, and Meyer 2002).

Possible changes in soil organic matter (SOM) and their relationship with nutrient status are poorly understood, despite their importance in sustainable crop production. In a study made by Canellas et al. (2010), samples were taken in two areas, one where the sugar cane has been burnt at harvest since 1946 and a second where it has been left unburned throughout the same period. The study site was located in the municipality of Campos dos Goytacazes, Rio de Janeiro State, on a flat uniform area. The location had an average annual long-term rainfall of 1080 mm and a mean annual temperature of 24-25°C. The two plots sampled in the study were adjacent to each other. When their soil organic matter and nutrient pools were evaluated it was shown that management without burning promotes changes in SOM that induce the accumulation of aromatic C, humins, and humic acid fractions, thereby increasing the hydrophobic character of the stable organic matter to at least 40 cm in the soil examined. In addition, the content of labile N, P, and sulphur (S) compounds was also higher in the soils where the cane had not been burnt, suggesting that the preservation of different labile compounds within the hydrophobic domains of SOM can protect against rapid microbial degradation.

These results highlight the importance of agricultural practices that lead to a relative increase of SOM-hydrophobic domains as a key mechanism for enhancing labile forms of macronutrients and preventing rapid microbial degradation, generating conservative management for nutrient recycling processes, and thereby contributing to sustainable soil fertility.

MECHANICAL HARVESTING

In the future, mechanical harvesting will be more and more common in developed countries like Brazil. Since manual harvesting of sugar cane without burning is not economically feasible, mechanical harvesters that can collect the stalks and leave the residues in the fields have been developed. However, if the fields are burned prior to harvest, the cane can still be harvested by a combine harvester.

By 2014, 80% of the cane harvested in the main production regions in Brazil will be harvested without burning (Galdos et al. 2010). Mechanical harvesters are unpractical, however, in areas of small, irregular, and fragmented holdings, or where there are diversified cropping patterns, or where small farmers simply do not have sufficient resource capacity.

PRODUCTION OF CANE SUGAR

Traditional sugar cane processing involves two steps: first, the raw sugar is produced, and then it has to be refined. In the first step, the sweet juice is squeezed out from the washed, shredded stalks using steel rollers in the sugar mills. The squeezing process may be facilitated by the use of hot water or diluted hot cane juice. The raw extract is then clarified and neutralized, after which it is concentrated into syrup. Further concentration makes the syrup supersaturated and it starts to crystallize. Sugar is then separated from molasses by centrifugation. The refining process includes affination, decolouring, and crystallization. During affination, the outer coating of the sugar crystals is removed, and decolouring removes any coloured impurities. Evaporation of the purified syrup leads to the crystallization of sucrose, which is dried to produce refined sugar (Berlitz et al. 2004). New sugar mill technology makes it possible to produce white sugar directly from raw cane juice. This new technology eliminates the refining process by the use of membrane filtration, refrigeration, ion-exchange demineralization, and decolourization. This technology has already been introduced in Brazil (Jensen & Kitching 2008).

Producers will continue to try to find ways of enhancing the sugar yield from sugar cane production through selection of the most suitable varieties as well as through optimization of harvest methods and sugar production methods. In addition, we believe that there also will be an increased focus on the use of sugar cane for other purposes beside food.

BIBLIOGRAPHY

Bachchhav, S.M. (2005). Fertigation technology for increasing sugarcane production. *Indian Journal of Fertilizers*, vol. 1, pp. 85-89.
Bayer CropScience. (2010). Bayer CropScience extends sugarcane-research and teams up with the leading Brazilian sugar cane technology center CTC. *News Release*, pp. 1-3.

Berlitz, H.-D., Grosch, W., & Schieberle, P. (2004). *Food Chemistry*. Berlin, Heidelberg, New York: Springer, pp. 862-890.

Bloomberg. (2010, December 6). Brazil may increase Sugar exports by 20% this year Conab says. *San Francisco Chronicle*.

Canellas, L.P., Busato, J. G., Dobbs, L.B., Baldotto, M.A., Rumjanek, V.M., & Olivares, F.L. (2010). Soil organic matter and nutrient pools under long-term non-burning management of sugar cane. *European Journal of Soil Science*, vol. 61, pp. 375-383.

de Oliveira, A.L.M., Canuto, E.L., Urquiaga, S., Reis, V.M., & Baldani, J.I. (2006). Yield of micropropagated sugar cane varieties in different soil types following inoculation with diazotrophic bacteria. *Plant and Soil*, vol. 284, pp. 23-32.

ELLA Policy Brief. From manual to mechanical harvesting: reducing environmental impacts and increasing cogeneration potential. Retrieved from http://ella.practicalaction.org/node/1046 (June 2012).

FAOSTAT. Crop production. Food and Agriculture Organization of the United Nations. Retrieved from http://faostat.fao.org/site/567/DesktopDefault.aspx?PageID=567. (17.6.2010).

Galdos, M.V., Cerri, C.C., Lal, R., Bernoux, M., Feigl, B., & Cerri, C.E.P. (2010). Net greenhouse gas fluxes in Brazilian ethanol production systems. *GCB Bioenergy*, vol. 2, pp. 37-44.

Galvão, L.S., Formaggio, A.R., & Tisot, D.A. (2005). Discrimination of sugar cane varieties in Southeastern Brazil with EO-1 Hyperion data. *Remote Sensing of Environment*, vol. 94, pp. 523 534.

GMO Compass (2007). *GM sugarcane by end of decade*. Retrieved from www.gmo-compass. org (June 2012).

Graham, M.H., Hayes, R.J., & Meyer, J.H. (2002). Soil organic matter content and quality: effects of fertilizer applications, burning and thrash retention on a long-term sugar cane experiment in South Africa. *Soil Biology & Biochemistry*, vol. 34, pp. 93-102.

Halford, N.G., Curtis, T.Y., Muttucumaru, N., Postles, J., & Mottram, D.S. (2011). Sugars in crop plants. *Annals of Applied Biology*, vol. 158, pp. 1-25.

Hartemink, A.E. (2008). Sugarcane for bioethanol: Soil and environmental issues. *Advances in Agronomy*, vol. 99, pp. 125-172.

Jensen, C.R.C., & Kitching, S.M. (2008). Options for retrofitting white sugar milling (WSM) technology into existing raw sugar factories. *International Sugar Journal*, vol. 110, p 388.

Kackson, P.A. (2005). Breeding for improved sugar content in sugarcane. *Field Crops Research*, vol. 92, pp. 277-290.

Lingle, S.E., Johnson, R.M., Tew, T.L., & Viator, R.P. (2010). Changes in juice quality and sugarcane yield with recurrent selection for sucrose. *Field crops research*, vol. 118, pp. 152-157.

Netafim ACS Israel. (2011). Growing guidelines for sugarcane 2011. Retrieved from www. sugarcanecrops.com.

Wiedenfeld, R.P. (1995). Effects of irrigation and N fertilizer application on sugarcane yield and quality. *Field Crops Research*, vol. 43, pp. 101-108.

PART FOUR: THE ART OF SLAVERY

Opening Remarks

By Karen-Margrethe Simonsen

Slavery and modernity seem like contradictory terms. Yet the introduction of slavery to America from the early 16th century onwards went hand in hand with modernization. Especially in the sugar industry, slavery was organized according to a modern economic rationality and was even seen as a locomotive of modernity. Despite the inherent racism and the feudal, paternalistic structure of many sugar mills, these mills became the most modern industries not only in America but in the world. During the 17th and 18th centuries new technologies were introduced, such as steam engines, sugar-grinding machines, and railways, and right from the beginning the sugar industry was international. Not only did plantation owners buy slave-labourers abroad, the entire sugar industry was built on a transnational network of brokers, agents, and financers (Beckles, 1997: 778). The sugar mill owners were seen as "the incarnation of entrepreneurial freedom" and the spearheads of modernity; sugar as a product was the refined symbol of pure progress. In their own self-understanding and also in that of the world, the slave-owners were even seen as the kind of people that would secure the humanistic development of democracy. Eric Williams observed in the 1940s that the slave owners and the politicians who backed them up argued that enslavement was a means of helping black people achieve contact with civilization (Williams 1943: 70). Yet at the same time, these slave-owners incarnated medieval ideals of control and power.

The simultaneity and incongruence of modernity and slavery has often been pointed out as a paradox; it remains a riddle how ideas of humanism could thrive alongside any defence of slavery, even within the same discourse and person – even within great humanists like Thomas Jefferson, John Locke, and Immanuel Kant, who all had an undoubted impact on our philosophical and political understanding of democracy and modernity.

One way of understanding this 'paradox' is to point to the economic benefits of the slave-system that often led to moral self-contradictions, as Eric Williams has so brilliantly pointed out. But if we want to understand the complexities of slavery, we also have to look into how it was embedded in different local and national cultures. Although slavery was unequivocally an evil, understandings of slavery and cultural encounters in sugar plantations varied a great deal. Aside from all the gruesome stories of brutality, the most surprising thing, seen from a modern standpoint, is that the sugar mill was often romanticized by both whites and blacks, and seen as a model of Christian communality where blacks interacted with whites under the caring supervision of a benevolent 'father.'

Even if we cannot agree with such a romanticized view, it is an historical fact that sugar mills were melting pots that despite social hierarchy managed to blend black cultures with other black cultures with different white cultures. This blending happened on both cultural and biological levels and it gradually came to influence and transform the cultural identity not only of the persons involved but of the entire nations. Through this hybridization, another kind of global modernity appeared that can arguably be seen as more modern than the technological advances of the age, since it was a premonition of a global hybrid culture that came to light much later.

This has been pointed out by Fernando Ortiz in Cuba and Gilberto Freyre in Brazil. Life in the sugar industry generated a transcultural reality which established hybridity as a multifaceted norm that despite its harsh origins became a positive building block of a real modernity.

In the following two chapters, we have chosen to focus on sugar and slavery in Cuba and Brazil. These two countries are especially interesting because they were the first to introduce slavery at the beginning of the 16th century and the last to abolish it. England abolished slavery in her Caribbean colonies in the early 1830s; France did the same in 1848. Cuba did not abolish slavery until 1886, and in Brazil it took until 1888 (Bergad 2007: xii). Cuba and Brazil thus have long and varied histories of slavery. They were also two of the colonies that imported the most slaves – Brazil in particular was the leading slave-importer for more than 250 years, totalling more than 34% of all slaves ever imported (Bergad 2007: 62).

Slaves were used in very different kinds of work and there were many differences in their conditions. But slavery in the sugar industry has become a kind of archetype of slavery. Work on the sugar plantations was extraordinarily hard, and there was a high death rate and low fertility. Slavery in sugar plantations is often mentioned as the most dramatic and harshest kind of slavery, but it was in the sugar plantations that the greatest transcultural exchange occurred and technological modernity advanced most quickly.

Taking into consideration that in Cuba and Brazil slavery lasted for more than 400 years, it is remarkable how few testimonies we have from this period; North America, for example, produced many more. But the focus here is not on firsthand testimony; we have chosen to focus on two literary writers who have contributed to the general cultural reception of slavery following its abolition. These two writers thematize slavery in very different ways.

José Lins do Rego (1901-1957) was a novelist whose origins were in the sugar cane plantations in the northeast of Brazil. As a participant of the modernist movement in Brazil, he is known as one of the leading regional figures of Brazilian Literature in the 20th century. His sugar cane cycle gives a critical portrait of life in the plantation over the course of five novels. These novels, written between 1932 and 1936, cover the first years of the 20th century and provide vivid portrayals of plantation life both when a sugar mill was a paternalistic family business and when it became a modern industry. A significant aspect of Rego's sugar cane cycle is that it describes a post-slavery society in which slavery is still the defining institution.

Nicolás Guillén (1902-1989) was a Cuban poet of mixed African and Spanish descent. He played an enormous role in pre-and post-revolutionary Cuba and became the national poet under Castro. He was very interested in traditional African legend, literary form, and music and combined some of these elements into his poetry, which is extraordinarily sonorous and at the same time full of images of social life and political critique of the power forms in both traditional sugar plantations and modern capitalism.

Nicolás Guillén and José Lins do Rego were contemporaries but there are big differences in their styles and their approaches to slavery. However, they share the idea that an understanding of the roots and nature of slavery can contribute to an understanding of modernity. Without an understanding of the cultural roots and hybrid cultures of the sugar plantations, it is impossible to understand the development of the countries they write about.

The following two chapters ask questions about the kind of symbolic content sugar had as a product in the cultural context of slavery and the kind of modernity that was created in nations where the sugar industry and slavery played significant roles in development.

BIBLIOGRAPHY

Beckles, H.M. (1997). Capitalism, Slavery and Caribbean modernity. *Callaloo*, vol. 20, issue 4, pp. 777-789.

Bergad, L.W. (2007). *The Comparative Histories of Slavery in Brazil, Cuba and the United States*. Cambridge: Cambridge University Press.

Gilberto, F. (1970). *The Masters and the Slaves. A Study in the Development of Brazilian Civilization*. New York: Alfred A. Knopf.

Ortiz, F. (1995). *Cuban Counterpoint. Tobacco and Sugar*. Durham and London: Duke University Press.

Williams, E. (1943). Laissez faire. Sugar and slavery. *Political Science Quarterly*, vol. 58, issue 1, pp. 67-85.

Williams, E. (1964). *Capitalism and Slavery*. London: Andre Deutsch.

CHAPTER VII

The Perceptions of Modernity in José Lins do Rego's Sugar Cane Cycle, or "not all sugar is sweet"

By Vinicius Mariano de Carvalho

There have been sugar plantations in the northeast region of Brazil ever since the beginning of the Portuguese presence in the New World. Sugar cane was introduced to the country in the 16th century by the Portuguese, who realised that the new land was perfect for it. According to Mintz, "By 1526, Brazil was shipping sugar to Lisbon in commercial quantities, and soon the sixteenth century was the Brazilian century for sugar" (Mintz 1985: 33). But the "engenhos" (sugar mills) became more than an economic resource, as they set the scene for the development of a particular culture. This sugar cane culture, especially in the provinces of Pernambuco, Alagoas, and Paraíba, changed the natural landscape and gave a peculiar face to Brazilian society in the northeast – a society founded on slavery, where only the white colonisers had a voice and rights.

By the end of the 19th century, sugar cane plantations had been completely restructured in northeast Brazil. The end of slavery, the introduction of taxation on the trade of the sugar, and the modernisation of sugar production together broke the traditional and pre-modern model of plantation society. The "engenho" became a symbol of a failed society, and this crisis in adapting to a new and modern model forced a reconfiguration of the culture.

The change in the logics of production from a pre-modern model to a modern one reconfigured the society that was built around the sugar cane plantations. Change also occurred in these communities' perceptions of life. In the pre-modern model of sugar production and the society organised around it, the sugar was considered blessed because the world appeared to revolve around its plantation, production, and consumption. However, in the new and modern model of the production, all social structures broke down and sugar became a curse. The power of sugar catalysed the meeting of different cultures in northeast Brazil, but the expansion of this power also broke cultural ties. The discourse of modernity as synonymous with progress and development is here contradicted: the society that was born after the modernisation of sugar production opened up a deep socioeconomic gap that eventually led to severe cultural disruption in northeast Brazil.

By the beginning of the 20th century, the sugar cane regions in northeast Brazil had become the setting for two different cultural, social and economic perceptions. On one side, the "engenho" represented a pre-modern model. It was more than a sugar refinery; it was a social and cultural construction, intertwined with various colonial structures and the heirs of the tradition of slavery. In this pre-modern perception, sugar was a symbol of blessing. Life was organised around the plantation, the harvest, and the milling of sugar cane. Social roles were understood, and the world seemed pre-ordained. Of course, sugar was not a "blessing" for everybody, considering the fact that this pre-modern model of production in the "engenhos" was based on slavery. The end of slavery and the modernisation of sugar production did not, however, bring social development to the region. The shift from the pre-modern model to the modern model disrupted the social amalgam of the northeast region. Former slaves were not integrated economically into the labour market and remained subject to inhuman treatment. So while modernity generally represents opportunities for social, political and personal advancement, liberating people from the oppressiveness of the past, the modernisation of the sugar cane society of northeast Brazil was a different story. Progress in production methods did not offer those living in the plantation society new perspectives on the sharing of goods.

It is in this context of two very different perceptions of the world that the Brazilian literary movement known as Regionalism appeared during the 1930s. Regionalism aimed to restore the traditional values of northeast Brazil, especially those of the culture that had developed around the sugar cane plantations and sugar production. This movement, characteristically conservative, tends to view modernity as the disruption of a world in balance and celebrates an idyllic pre-modern world in which sugar was a blessing.

The ideological mentor of this movement was the Brazilian sociologist Gilberto Freyre. Several writers with north-eastern origins joined the movement and Regionalism became one of the most important literary movements of the 20th century in Brazil. José Lins do Rêgo is considered one of its most prominent writers. The five novels of his sugar cane cycle are widely recognised as the model for the regionalist novel. In the following, we will describe the key aspects of the Regionalist movement and analyse Rego's sugar cane cycle in the light of the question about how northeast Brazil's transition into modernity should be perceived.

REGIONALISM

Regionalism was one of the most important literary movements in Brazilian modernism. *A Bagaceira*, by José Américo de Almeida (1930), is considered to be one of the first Brazilian novels to incorporate regional material in its composition in a systematic manner, trying to provide a realistic portrait of the men of the hinterland. Novels from northeast Brazil in particular began to have a more social approach, describing the political, cultural, social, and economic problems of the region. This is also reflected in the language of these novels, which attempts to reproduce the regional colloquial speech; at times the result is slightly caricatured, but the attempt indicates a general concern with the value of the cultural traditions of a decaying world.

The cyclic quality of these novels revealed an aspect of the countryside that had been ignored by the literary centres of Rio de Janeiro and São Paulo, and which was highly important to the notion known as the "discovering of Brazil." After 1922 the modernists attempted to "discover" an archaic, pre-modern, primitive Brazil. It is interesting to observe that Regionalism, with its emphasis on a sort of nostalgia for pre-modern society, developed within the modernist movement of Brazilian literature.

In the works of Gilberto Freyre, and especially in *The Masters and the Slaves: A study in the development of Brazilian civilization* and *The Mansions and the Shanties: The making of modern Brazil*, the necessity of resurrecting and preserving selected elements of the past is emphasised. Freyre claims that this is the only way of avoiding the total cultural monotony caused by modernity. The central thesis in Freyre's sociological model was the idea of "lusotropicalism," which considers miscegenation a positive aspect of the Portuguese colonisation of Brazil. To Freyre, slavery on the Brazilian plantations was less despotic than in the US, for instance, and there was a higher degree of integration among the Portuguese colonisers that enabled them to establish cordial ways in their power over the slaves. In this "acclimatization" we see the roots of the north-eastern culture, and this culture is precisely what the Regionalism movement aimed to preserve.[1]

In 1926, Freyre organised a *Congresso Regionalista* (Regionalist Conference) in Recife with the goal of revaluing the cultural heritage of northeast Brazil, which was threatened by the emergence of new values arising from the process of modernisation. According to José Luiz Ferreira (2010: 115-116):

> o fato desencadeador de toda aquela discussão foi, reiteramos, o acelerado processo de decadência da região e as conseqüentes mudanças advindas do processo de modernização, que exigiam a mecanização do processo de produção do açúcar e, atrelado a essa mecanização, um novo modelo de trabalho e de relações sociais.[2]

Regionalism can be understood as a conservative reaction by the local intelligentsia to an economic and social modernisation, which was happening in Recife as well as the rest of northeast Brazil around at that time. Protected ideologically and aesthetically by the modernist movement, this group of Regionalists founded a justification for a new literary voice in the context of Brazilian literature. A voice, according to this group that gathered itself around Freyre, which was able show a Brazil that had been forgotten by the urban centres of Rio de Janeiro and São Paulo. The key precepts of Regionalism were reinforced in the *Manifesto Regionalista*,[3] by Freyre:

---

1   Freyre's efforts to rehabilitate the idea of a pacific miscegenation of black culture with the Portuguese colonisers as well as identifying Brazil as a conciliatory country is comparable to similar attempts by other Latin American writers such as those of Fernando Ortiz in Cuba (*Contrapunteo Cubano de Tobacco y Azúcar*, 1940) and José Vasconcelos in Mexico (*La Raza Cosmica*, 1926).

2   "The trigger of that whole discussion was, we reiterate, the accelerated decay of the region and the consequent changes resulting from the modernization process, which required the mechanization of the sugar production process and, coupled to this mechanization, a new work and social relations model."

3   The *Manifesto Regionalista* was first published in 1952, but according to Freyre, it was written and read at the First Brazilian Congress of Regionalism, celebrated in Recife in February 1926. The text begins with the most important aims of the movement: "Há dois ou três anos que se esboça nesta velha metrópole regional que é o Recife um movimento de reabilitação de valores regionais e tradicionais desta parte do Brasil." ("For the last two or three years in this old regional metropolis, Recife, we have seen the development of a movement that seeks to rehabilitate regional and traditional values of this part of Brazil.")

Procuramos defender esses valores e essas tradições, isto sim, do perigo de serem de todo abandonadas, tal o furor neófilo de dirigentes que, entre nós, passam por adiantados e "progressistas" pelo fato de imitarem cega e desbragadamente a novidade estrangeira. A novidade estrangeira de modo geral. De modo particular(...) o que o Rio ou São Paulo consagram como "elegante" e como "moderno".[4] (Freyre 1996: 48)

This statement makes obvious the reaction against the modernisation that had been taking place in Brazil since the first years of the 20th century. The only way to preserve the traditions of the old (and mythological) northeast Brazil was deliberately to promote a cultural movement that could save a tradition in danger of being abandoned because of modernisation.

The sugar cane plantations, sugar production, and the culture developed around them all had important roles in the traditions that Freyre wanted to preserve. According to Freyre, sugar was much more than just an economic commodity; it was responsible for the definition of the first character of Brazil. In his words:

Sem se julgar estultamente o sul do Brasil, mas apenas o seu maior e melhor produtor de açúcar nos tempos coloniais – açúcar que está à base de uma doçaria rica como nenhuma, do Império, e à base, também, de uma doce aristocracia de maneiras de gostos, de modos de viver e de sentir, tornada possível pela produção e exportação de um mascavo tão internacionalmente famoso como, depois, o café de São Paulo – o Nordeste tem o direito de considerar-se uma região que já grandemente contribuiu para dar a cultura ou à civilização brasileira autenticidade e originalidade e não apenas doçura ou tempero.[5] (Freyre 1996: 49)

---

4   "We seek to defend these values and traditions from the danger of being abandoned by our leaders with neophyle furor who pretend to be advanced and progressive while imitating blindly and shamelessly the novelty of the foreign. All sorts of foreign novelty Especially those (foreign novelty) considered as 'elegant' and 'modern' in Rio or São Paulo."

5   "Without foolishly judging the south of Brazil, but only its highest and best producer of sugar in colonial times – sugar that is the basis of rich desserts like no others from the Imperial time, and also the base of a sweet aristocracy of manners, tastes, ways of living and feeling. This aristocracy was made possible by the production and export of brown sugar, internationally famous as later the coffee from São Paulo. Considering this, the Brazilian northeast has the right to be considered a region that greatly contributed to give authenticity and originality to the Brazilian culture and civilization and not just sweetness or spice."

In other words, to Freyre, the culture that grew up around the production of sugar was a real civilisation, original and strong. The aim of the Regionalism movement was to preserve this culture. However, somehow Freyre did not want to see that in order to succeed in preserving this civilization, he would have to maintain a pre-modern society based on slavery. His romantic view of the slavery-based society in Brazil determines his analyses and justifies the idea of sugar as a blessing. For Freyre, the modernisation of the production of sugar in the northeast destroyed a peaceful and harmonious society and failed to bring any new benefits to the people. He even considers that the end of slavery might have brought more problems to the former slaves. In another work dedicated to the subject of sugar in the northeast, Freyre declares:

A verdade é que talvez em nenhuma outra região do Brasil a extinção do regime de trabalho escravo tenha significado tão nitidamente como no Nordeste da cana-de-açúcar a degradação das condições de vida do trabalhador rural e do operário. A degradação do homem. Da assistência ao escravo – assistência social, moral, religiosa, e até médica, que bem ou mal era praticada pela maioria dos senhores escravocratas no interesse das próprias terras, da própria lavoura, do próprio açúcar, da própria família (…) – quase não resta senão um traço ou outro, uma ou outra tradição mais sentimental do que efetiva, nos engenhos mais velhos, em uma ou em outra usina de senhor menos ausente do campo.

A industrialização e principalmente a comercialização da propriedade rural vem criando usinas possuídas de longe, algumas delas por fulano ou sicrano & companhia, firmas para as quais os cabras trabalham sem saber direito para quem, quase sem conhecer senhores, muito menos senhoras.[6] (Freyre 2004: 177)

---

6   "The truth is that perhaps in no other region of Brazil as clearly as in the Northeast of the sugar cane the extinction of slave labor has meant the degradation of living conditions for the peasant and the worker. The degradation of man. Hardly a trace remains of the social, moral, religious, and medical assistance that was well or poorly given to the slaves by their owners. Assistance not because the owners were worried about the slaves, but on behalf of their own land, their own farming, their own sugar, their own family … Some traces of this assistance, tradition more sentimental than effective, remains merely in some old mills, where the owners are still present on the plantations.

Industrialization and commercialization of rural property has been creating factories owned by unknowns, some of them by so-and-so & Company, firms for which the workers work without knowing for whom, almost without knowing the owners, much less their wives."

Now that we have considered the ideological and aesthetical bases of the Regionalist movement and its nostalgic compromise with a pre-modern model of society, represented by the sugar cane civilisation of northeast Brazil, we can turn our attention to Rego's sugar cane cycle. The cycle deals with the world of plantation in the Paraíba Province. Our aim is to try to observe the ways in which his novels were responsible for on the one hand a fixation with an idyllic sugar cane society (following the recipe of Freyre's Regionalist Manifesto), and, on the other hand, a demonstration of how the modernisation of this society is essentially a failure precisely because it was originally founded on a failed process of production based on slavery.

JOSÉ LINS DO REGO AND THE SUGAR CANE CYCLE

Rego was born in the village of Pilar, in the same province as Paraiba, in 1901. He was the son and grandson of plantation owners. His early years on his grandfather's plantation became the richly re-created background of the novels in which he outlined the splendour and decay of the sugar plantation. He studied law in Recife, where he was closely associated with other important intellectuals. Much influenced by the writing and ideas of the sociologist Gilberto Freyre, he became one of the most prominent representatives of literary Regionalism. In 1924 he moved to Rio de Janeiro, where he continued to write prolifically. Altogether, in the 25 years between 1932 and 1957, Lins do Rego published 23 novels. The first five, *Menino de Engenho* (1932), *Doidinho* (1933), *Bangüê* (1934), *O Moleque Ricardo* (1935), and *Usina* (1936), together constitute the sugar cane cycle. Several years later, he published *Fogo Morto* (1943) and his last work, *Meus Verdes Anos* (1956). Though they represent a discontinuity in relation to the novels of the sugar cane cycle, these two last novels are considered by some critics to be part of the cycle because of their common theme.

The sugar cane cycle reveals several aspects of the sugar cane culture in northeast Brazil, tracing portraits of the types of people found in this region and the ways in which they were affected by the modernisation of sugar production in the early years of the 20th century. In many ways, Rego recovers his own history and this gives a deep autobiographical accent to his novels. The following presents an overview of each of the novels in the cycle.

The first, *Menino de Engenho*, was published in 1932. It describes life in the traditional "engenhos" (sugar mills) and the power of the "Senhor de engenho." The main character and narrator, Carlinhos, is the grandson of the "Senhor do engenho." He grows up in the sugar mill and the narrative is based on his childhood memories. Sugar production is absolutely central to the order of life in the mill, and this pre-modern logic prevails in the narrator's perception of the world. It is important to remember that these are the memories of a child, so the point of view of the narrative is almost naïve in many aspects regarding the conditions of life for many inhabitants of the "engenho." It is even more important to observe that for the narrator, the "engenho" represents a self-contained world in which the "Senhor do engenho" is likened to God: he holds the power to organise the entire world in his hands. Everybody is under his protection and the only thing that he cannot control is nature.

The year after, 1933, Rego published *Doidinho*, a continuation of *Menino de Engenho*. This novel represents a clash between two worlds: the pre-modern logic meets the modern logic. Carlinhos is sent to a school in the city, where he encounters a very different world from that of the sugar mill, where everything had seemed organised and in perfect balance. To be accepted in this new world, he tries to deny the "engenho" in order to leave pre-modernity and become modern. The title of the book, *Doidinho* ("little mad boy"), which is also Carlinhos' nickname, represents his situation very well.

Bangüê, the third novel in the cycle published in 1934, details the return of Carlinhos to the "engenho" and the impossibility of combining the two worlds, the pre-modern and the modern. It depicts the fragmentation of the human being in parallel to the fragmentation of the "engenho." The economic decadence of the sugar mill and the death of the "Senhor de engenho," Carlinhos's grandfather, contribute to the disruption of the pre-modern society, which was only kept in balance by the symbolic power of the "senhor." Carlinhos is a picture of this decadent and meaningless world. Unable to manage the "engenho" with the same power as his grandfather, confronted with the impossibility of living his great love for Maria Alice, a married woman, and frustrated in his intellectual ambitions, Carlinhos leads the "engenho" to become a "bangüê" (a sort of mill of small dimensions in which the machines are powered by animals). This fragmentation is not only personal, but extends to society at large. The novel ends with Carlinhos leaving the engenho and returning to the city.

The 1935 novel *O Moleque Ricardo* is quite different from the others in the cycle, since it represents the point of view of the oppressed. Ricardo, a poor black man born in same "engenho" as Carlinhos, also tries to deny his fate and enter the modern model of society. Though he was born after the end of the slavery, his living conditions in the "engenho" were similar to that of his slave ancestors. He escapes to the city, the symbol of modernity, to try to build a new life, but his attempt is not successful. The book represents the failure of the integration of the two logics, this time from the perspective of the oppressed. Ricardo is a counterpoint to Carlinhos: they grew up together in the engenho, they used to play together as children, but Ricardo is the face of the oppressed, while Carlinhos is the face of the power.

The plot of *O Moleque Ricardo* could be read as conforming with Freyre's theory about how the end of slavery broke the balance in the sugar cane society; it is indeed a penetrating analysis of the conflict caused by modernization in the region since it merely reproduced the oppression of slavery in the conditions of workers. In this novel, Rego introduces political matters concerning the life of workers in the city. Strikes, unions, and the beginning of communism in northeast Brazil are well drawn by the author. It is important to stress, however, that even in the city, here a symbol of modernity, the society and economy revolves around sugar production, which is always seen as the centre of the region's affairs. The novel ends with Ricardo been sent to prison on Fernando de Noronha Island, because of his involvement in a failed political coup.

Usina, the last novel in the cycle, published in 1936, is a paradigmatic novel of Brazilian literature. It begins as a continuation of *Moleque Ricardo*, narrating his life in prison and his release. It is probably the first Brazilian novel in which a homosexual relationship is not pictured as morally improper. As a prisoner, Ricardo is able to experience real love with another prisoner. Although there is much to be said about this aspect of the narrative, what interests us in this essay is Ricardo's release from the prison and his return to the "engenho." Disappointed with his experience in the modern city environment and removed from the balanced and fulfilling life that he had lived in prison, Ricardo tries to return to his origins, to a pre-modern world that no longer exists. Back in the "engenho" he witnesses the complete dismemberment of that model of society. The "engenho" is sold and the factories (*usinas*) take possession of everything, evicting the people who used to live and work there. There is a symbolic element to this replacement: as the "usina" replaces the "engenho", the modern replaces the pre-modern. Sugar production increases, but, at same time, the plantation of sugar cane disrupts the life of the people. Ricardo's attempts to recover the balance actually get him involved in riots. Sugar, which has always been seen as a blessing, becomes a curse, disrupting equilibrium in all aspects: socially, economically, and ecologically. At the end of the novel, the "usina" is destroyed by flooding along with the whole sugar plantation. Decades before any discussion of ecology, Rego already recognizes the risks of the monoculture of sugar cane and the damage it can cause to human lives.

SUGAR: THE MAIN CHARACTER

Rego's sugar cane cycle has always been cited as the best description of life in the sugar society of northeast Brazil. In a study from 1952, the critic Alvaro Lins states that "nestas páginas, aliás, encontramos alguma coisa mais do que o drama de um personagem: a síntese da biografia de um engenho nordestino" (Lins 1952: 9).[7] Otto Maria Carpeaux, another eminent literary critic, adds:

> Pode-se dizer que José Lins do Rego é a expressão literária da cultura da sua terra; é mais da terra do que dos livros. É a consciência literária da casa-grande e da senzala, dos senhores de engenho e dos pretos, dos bacharéis e dos moleques, de todo um mundo agonizante.[8] (Carpeaux 1952: 20)

Curiously, Carpeaux refers to Rego's novels with the same terminology used by Freyre and, more than this, he accepts Freyre's dualistic description of northeast Brazil. The methodological use of antithetical pairs to explain Brazil's sugar society is central to Freyre's analysis. Thomson is more direct in establishing the correlation between Rego's novels and Freyre's sociology when he affirms that "Suas obras (Rego) sobre a vida do Nordeste constituem penetrante análise sociológica das condições sob as quais vivem e morrem milhões de brasileiros" (Thomson 1952: 3).[9]

This association between Freyre's sociology and Rego's literature became a commonplace in literary analysis in Brazil. While this association is broadly justified, considering the deep influence of Freyre on the regionalist writers of the 1930s, it limited the ways in which Rego's was read, especially in the

---

7   "On these pages, in fact, we find something more than the drama of a character: a summary of the biography of a Northeast sugar-cane mill."

8   "It could be said that José Lins do Rego is the literary expression of the culture of his land; it is more a literary expression of the land than the books. It is the literary conscience of the *Casa-grande* and the *Senzala* (slave quarters), of the mill owners and the blacks, of the *Bacharéis* (Lawyers) and the kids, of a whole dying world."

9   "Rego's works about life in the Northeast are a deeply sociological analysis of the conditions under which millions of Brazilians live and die."

case of the sugar cane cycle. Criticism of Rego's works has been contaminated with Freyre's sociology much more than the novels ever were. It was almost too easy to fit them together.[10]

Ivan Bichara Sobreira was the first to point out other ways in which the cycle may be read. In 1977 he wrote:

> quando em certos resumos literários, se fala no romance nordestino, e particularmente, no romance de José Lins do Rego, acentua-se, de logo, o traço predominante da sua obra: o registro, a análise, o estudo dos problemas sociais e econômicos do chamado ciclo da cana de açúcar. (...) José Lins do Rego se firmava como o romancista da realidade, do social, uma espécie de cronista da fecunda aventura do mestre Gilberto Freyre nos domínios da sociologia. Nada menos exato do que essa rígida classificação.[11] (Bichara 1977: 49)

Sobreira was right in pointing out that the sugar cane cycle was much more than just a chronicle of reality. This attitude was responsible for the dismissal of Rego's literature in some quarters that considered it blind to social problems, merely the nostalgic musings of a descendant of a "senhor de engenho." Without wholly disregarding the Freyre's influence on the cycle, but placing it as a backdrop, we can see an ensemble of novels in which the main character is not Carlinhos, his grandfather, Ricardo, or the "engenho," but simply the sugar. Around sugar, a tyrannical pre-modern society was built; because of sugar, slavery is introduced and families are submitted to an owner who is comparable to God in his power over them. In the name of sugar this society is broken by the liberation of the slaves and another society emerges. This new society, moving towards modernity, is merely a continuation of an unbalanced, disruptive, and thoroughly human process. Rego's sugar cane cycle is a chronicle of one frame of an endless history of an eternal character: sugar.

---

10   Reinforcing this sociological or historical interpretation of Rego's works, studies have recently appeared by Albuquerque, Dabat, and Ferreira, among others. All of them are meticulous analyses in their fields, but their perspective on Rego's Sugar Cane Cycle involves reading it as a historical or sociological document rather than as a literary work.

11   "When in certain literary summaries the subject is the northeastern novel, and particularly the novels by José Lins do Rego, what is stressed as the predominant aspect of his work is his record, his analysis, and his study of social and economic problems of the so-called sugar cane cycle. ... José Lins do Rego took hold as the novelist of the reality, the social, as a sort of chronicler of the fruitful adventures of the master Gilberto Freyre in the fields of sociology. Nothing is less accurate than this rigid classification."

Curiously, José Lins do Rego returns to this character later on in his career with two other works. The first is the novel *Fogo Morto*, from 1943, in which the world of the sugar cane cycle is revived in the same landscape of "engenho", with the same characters and themes of the sugar cane cycle, reinforcing the idea proposed here that the main character is actually sugar itself – ubiquitous, almighty, if not explicitly personified as a divine figuration. The great novelist's last work is the autobiographical *Meus Verdes Anos*, from 1956, which shares startling coincidences with some chapters of his first novel, *Menino de Engenho*. It is as if Rego inserts himself as a minor character into the endless narrative of sugar. He positions himself in this plot, as author and as character, in the passage from pre-modernity to modernity facing something far more powerful even than his own creativity: the sugar.

BIBLIOGRAPHY

Albuquerque, Jr. (2009). *A invenção do Nordeste e outras artes*. São Paulo: Cortez.

de Andrade, M.C. (1980). *The Land and People of Northeast Brazil*. (D.V. Johnson, Trans.). Albuquerque: University of New Mexico Press.

Carpeaux, O.M. (1952). José Lins do Rego. In *Cadernos de cultura*. Ministério da Educação e Saúde.

Coutinho, A. (Org.) (1991). *José Lins do Rego*. Rio de Janeiro: Civilização Brasileira, Coleção Fortuna Crítica, Volume 7.

Dabat, C.R. (2008). A *Canção de Rolando* e o *Ciclo da Cana-de-Açúcar*: dos usos da literatura na construção da história oficial. *Cadernos de História: Oficina de História. Revista do Dept. de História da UFPE*, vol. 5, issue 5, pp. 117-140. Recife: Ed. Universitária UFPE.

Fereira, J.L. (2010). Gilberto Freyre e Câmara Cascudo: perspectivas do elemento regional. In H.H. Araujo & I. T. Oliveira (Eds.), *Regionalismo, Modernização e Crítica Social na Literatura Brasileira*. São Paulo: Nankin.

Freyre, G. (2007). *Açúcar. Uma sociologia do doce, com receitas de bolos e doces do nordeste do Brasil*. São Paulo: Global.

Freyre, G. (1996). *Manifesto regionalista*. Recife: FUNDAJ, Ed. Massangana.

Freyre, G. (2004). *Nordeste*. Aspectos da Influência da Cana sobre a Vida e a Paisagem do Nordeste do Brasil. São Paulo: Global.

Freyre, G. (1956). *Terres du Sucre*. Trans. J. Orecchioni. Paris: Gallimard.

Mintz, S.W. (1985). *Sweetness and Power. The Place of Sugar in Modern History*. New York, Penguin Books.

Lins, A. (1952). José Lins do Rego. Um novo romance dos engenhos. In *Cadernos de cultura*. Ministério da Educação e Saúde.

do Rego, J.L. (2009). *Menino de Engenho*. Rio de Janeiro: José Olympio.

do Rego, J.L. (2008). *Doidinho*. Rio de Janeiro: José Olympio.

do Rego, J.L. (1978). *Bangüê*. Rio de Janeiro: José Olympio.

do Rego, J.L. (2008). *O Moleque Ricardo*. Rio de Janeiro: José Olympio.

do Rego, J.L. (2000). *Usina*. Rio de Janeiro: José Olympio.

do Rego, J.L. (1996). *Fogo Morto*. Rio de Janeiro: José Olympio.

do Rego, J.L. (1966). *Plantation Boy* [English translation of *Menino de Engenho*, *Doidinho* e *Bangüê*]. (E. Baum, Trans.). New York: Alfred A. Knopf.

do Rego, J.L. (1957). *Presença do nordeste na literatura*. Serviço de documentação. Ministério da Educação e Cultura – os Cadernos de Cultura, p 104.

Sobreira, I.B. (1977). *O romance de José Lins do Rego*. João Pessoa: editora universitária UFPB.

Thompsom, F. (1952). M. José Lins do Rego. In *Cadernos de cultura*. Ministério da Educação e Saúde.

CHAPTER VIII

"Sin azúcar no hay país": Transcultural Images of Sugar and Modernity in the Poetry of Nicolás Guillén

By Karen-Margrethe Simonsen

"It did not take long for sugar to become everything.
[...] sugar has never encountered a
sustained counterdiscourse in Cuba."
(Benítez Rojo 1986: 13)

In Cuba, there used to be a popular saying: "sin azúcar no hay país" ("without sugar there is no country"). This chapter begins by asking what it means to say that the existence of a country depends on the existence of sugar. How can sugar *create* a nation, or in Benedict Anderson's term, an "imagined community"? And how did sugar become such a strong discourse that according to Antonio Benítez Rojo, it was able to eradicate all possible counterdiscourses? I have looked for answers in two places: in Fernando Ortiz's important book *Contrapunteo cubano del tabaco y el azúcar* from 1940; and in Cuban literature, mainly from the 19th century and the beginning of the 20th century. In this chapter, I will concentrate on the role of sugar in the poetry of Nicolás Guillén (born 1902). In earlier poetry from the 19th century, for instance in the poetry of El Cucalambé, another immensely popular poet, the simple rural life of the sugar plantations is related to the original paradisiacal life of the native Ciboney people. However, most literary works during the 19th century that treat the issue of sugar do so in its relation to slavery. This is also the case in the much later poetry of Nicolás Guillén, but despite the dominance of the theme of slavery, sugar, sugar cane, and sugar plantations play vital and sometimes even positive roles in his poetry.

Before my discussion of the motif of sugar in some selected poems by Guillén, a couple of things need to be said about the special situation of the Cuban nation in a modern global context.

In Cuba, the explosive growth of the sugar industry in the 19th century coincided with the growth of nationalism.[1] It is partly this coincidence that explains the dominance of sugar in the national imagery of Cuba. The industry expanded dramatically but it would be a mistake to attribute the cultural importance of sugar simply to how much was produced. Sugar played such an important role not only because of the scale of production but because many of the country's most important cultural issues were negotiated through discussions about sugar. For many years, sugar-related issues were at the heart of all economic, legal, and cultural exchange inside Cuba and between Cuba and the world. This is another reason why sugar became one of the central elements in Fernando Ortiz's development of the influential concept of *transculturation*.

Ortiz published his book *Contrapunteo cubano del tabaco y el azúcar* (*Cuban Counterpoint: Tobacco and Sugar*) in 1940. He argues that sugar and tobacco not only contributed significantly to Cuba's economic development, they also functioned as "protagonists" in Cuban history and cultural metaphors for oppositional elements in Cuban modernity (Ortiz 1940: 137). While sugar has been associated with imported white culture, especially Spanish colonialism, the slave trade, and mechanization, tobacco has often been associated with original, "mystical" Indian culture.

Sugar and tobacco can be opposed to each other, but they are also contradictory within themselves. Though tobacco was originally grown and used by Indians, it was later mainly cultivated by Cubans with Spanish origins. Similarly, sugar is not only associated with Spanish colonialism but also with the hybrid culture of the sugar mills and plantations. The work force included not only black slaves of very different African origins but also Chinese. Both

---

1   The rapid development of the sugar industry in the 19th Century happened partly due to external causes, for instance the opening up of the market in the USA for Cuba; Spain's liberalizing trade reforms in the late 18th century; and especially the revolution in Haiti. Until the end of the 18th century, Haiti was the dominant sugar producing country in the area but the revolution caused a massive dip in production, which made the price of sugar go up and left the market open for Cuba (see Staten 2005: 11ff). Fernando Ortiz claims that the Cuban sugar industry did not grow significantly until after 1880, following the introduction of new steam-driven machinery. This is only relatively true. Seen from the perspective of 1940 (the time of Ortiz's book), when the sugar industry was much larger, production in the early 19th century may have seemed small; but in relation to production in the 18th century, the 19th century saw significant increases.

French and English people also worked here, the former often in charge of the chemical processes and the latter in charge of the machinery (Ortiz 2002: 237). This is what Ortiz calls "extranjerismo interno (*internal foreignness*)". Sugar production was regulated from the outside (by Spanish laws, American markets, etc.) but it also internalized foreign influences, naturalizing foreign elements and creating unique Cuban hybrids. Thus, the sugar mill worked as a transcultural machine, mixing many extremely different cultures. This does not mean that opposition and conflict were absent: transculturation does not eliminate political, economic, or social hierarchies and conflicts but rather it explains how different cultures interact and change within one social dynamic. According to Ortiz, transculturation can be understood as such:

> I am of the opinion that the word *Tranculturalizacíon* better expresses the different phases of the process of transition from one culture to another because this does not consist merely in acquiring another, which is what the English word *Acculturation* really implies but the process also necessarily involved the loss or uprooting of a previous culture which could be defined as a deculturation. In addition it carries the idea of the consequent creation of new cultural phenomena which could be neoculturation. (Ortiz 2002: 101).

Transculturation is therefore a complex, dynamic, unavoidable but painful negotiation of cultural identity. It is a sketchy, open-ended process that suffers from losses, suppressions, and gaps but also paves the way for potential richness of culture and progress. In contrast with a Hegelian understanding of development, for instance, transculturation works in a counter-dynamic (*contrapunteo*) way that can never be assimilated into smooth dialectics. The concept of transculturation underlines the fact that losses may continue to have an effect, even when they appear to have been overcome historically. Thus, transculturation opens up another way of regarding history: not as linear progress, but as development on the basis of spatial interactions, or the simultaneity of non-simultaneous elements. Because Cuba is a radical composite culture, transculturation is particularly evident here. As Ortiz writes: "The real history of Cuba is the history of its intermeshed transculturations" (Ortiz 2002: 98)

The study of the processes of transculturation in Cuba thus provides us with an image not only of the interaction between cultures but also an alternative way of understanding social modernity. It has often been pointed out that in Cuba (and to some extent in the whole of Latin America) there seems to be a discrepancy between technical modernity and social modernity. Thus,

Sybille Fischer in her remarkable book *Modernity Disavowed* claims both that Cuban society in the 19th century, including the processes of the slave trade, was extremely modern – as Stephen Mintz has said, more modern than Europe – *and* at the same time that this modernity "was not an ethos or a worldview that permeated society evenly, but rather a heterogeneous assemblage of strategies, effects, and forces that were brought into being by the operations of colonial power and enslavement" (Fischer 2004: 12). Modernity itself seems to be haunted by a heterogeneous logic of transculturation.

NATIONALISM AND LITERARY HISTORY

The history of literature in Cuba, just like the history of sugar, is closely connected with the period in the 19th century that saw both growing nationalism and the fight for independence (Llorens 1998: 7).[2] Literature in 19th-century Cuba was about determining *cubanidad*.

This project of nationalism presented a significant challenge in Cuba. Since the original inhabitants of the island died out leaving little or no trace of their culture, Cuban national identity had to be formed on the basis of immigrants of various sorts. Unlike almost any other nation in the 19th century, for Cuba there was no option of building on any surviving original culture.[3] Ortiz's book on Cuban identity does not take its point of departure in any specific ethnic group but in a mixture of ethnic groups, though he gives a special role to tobacco, a native plant that only the Indians knew how to smoke and that was known to form part of ancient religious rituals.

This mixture of ethnicities is also evident in Cuba's 19th- and 20th-century literature, during the period of national mythmaking. It is probably possible to distinguish between four different versions of Cuban national myths. Three of them understand mixed ethnicities to be a positive part of national identity, while the fourth recommends a purely white Cuba. But all four are based on

---

2   Indeed, in an interesting study, Irma Llorens claims that it is impossible to understand the history of nationalism in Cuba without reading the country's literature, just as it is impossible to understand the development of this literature without relating it to the rise of the nation (I. Llorens 1998: 7).

3   Some literary historians try to locate true Cubanness in the interior and eastern areas of Cuba, away from the coast and foreign influence (e.g. Lazo 1974). Others more recently have claimed that this distinction does not make sense and that all of Cuba and all the international influences on it have to be included in the definition of Cubanness (e.g. Pérez 1988; see Llorens 1998: 26 for a discussion of this).

different core identities, distinguished as: Indian; Black; White; Universalist. White nationalism was expressed for instance by José Antonio Saco in 1832 in an argument against the saccharocracy. Saco, who was a prominent intellectual and friend of Domingo del Monte, argued against the importation of any more slaves of African origin on the grounds that black people would contaminate the white Cuban race and the massive presence of people of African descent would impede the processes of modernization and democratization. Instead he recommended encouraging white workers to immigrate to Cuba.[4]

The universalist version is mainly represented by the hero of the independence war José Martí, who proclaimed the universal rights of all men as foundational for the new nation.

The Indian version was articulated by El Cucalambé. In his *Rumores de Hórmigo* from 1857, he mixes the original non-agricultural wildlife culture of the Ciboneys with the domesticated, primitive life of the labourers in the sugar cane plantations. The two cultures 'meet' in his poetry, or rather they are fused into one harmonious romantic vision of national unity.

Finally, Nicolás Guillén represents the 'black' national identity which is in reality both mixed and conflictual: there is no harmonious fusion between different racial identities but a dynamic history of intermeshing identities. Though he focuses on black identity, he does not essentialize it but inscribes it in a multifarious Cuban identity. "The spirit of Cuba is *mestizo*," he claims, "And from the spirit to the skin the definitive colour will come to us. Some day they will say: 'Cuban colour'."[5] Guillén is very much inspired by José Martí and his enlightened ideas of a humanistic, universal identity,[6] but in his writings it is the coloured complexity that is described as the ground of Cuban identity.

COLOURED NATION: NICOLÁS GUILLÉN

In his book *Contrapunteo cubano del azúcar y del tabaco*, Fernando Ortiz enumerates the many different characteristics of sugar and the sugar industry, including the nefarious aspect of colonialism and the slave trade. As mentioned above, many of the most important literary texts from 19th-century Cuba thematize explicitly the problem of the slave trade, for instance *Cecilie*

---

4   The aim was to "blanquear lo cubano" (Saco 1832; summarized in Benítez Rojo 1986: 21).

5   Quoted from the preface to *Sóngoro cosongo* (1931), here quoted from (Ellis 1983: 72).

6   See for instance Ellis's description of the inspiration that Guillén got from Martí and the many aspects they have in common (Ellis 1983: 198ff.).

Valdés (1839 and 1882) by Cirilo Villaverde and *Francisco, el ingenio, o las delicias del campo* (1838) by Anselmo Suárez y Romero. This concern is still prominent in the works of much later writers like Nicolás Guillén, for instance in his poem "Sweat and latigo":

Sudor y látigo

Látigo
sudor y látigo.
El sol despertó temprano,
y encontró al negro descalzo,
desnudo el cuerpo llagado,
sobre el campo.
Látigo,
sudor y látigo[7]

However, despite the awareness of the evils of slavery in Guillén's poetry, there is also a sense that such suffering can create a common destiny, as when he writes in the poem "Caña":

Caña

El negro
junto al cañaveral.

El yanqui
sobre el cañaveral.

La tierra
bajo el cañaveral.

Sangre
que se nos va![8]

---

7   "Sweat and latigo": "Latigo/Sweat and latigo./The sun rose early/and saw the barefoot negro/naked, the body bent/over the field/Latigo,/sweat and latigo/"

8   "Caña" in *Sóngoro cosongo*, 1994/1931. English translation: "Sugar cane": "The negro/ close to the sugar plantation/The yankee/above the sugar plantation/The earth/under the sugar plantation/Blood/ that escapes from us!"

In this remarkable poem, the opposition between black slave and white slave owner is recognized but the summarizing last sentence unites the two in a common destiny. It is also interesting that the title of the poem is simply "Sugar cane" rather than "Sugar plantation"; like the invocation of the earth in stanza three and the blood in stanza four, the title insists on the concreteness of this common destiny. The last "we" in stanza four can of course be read as a removed pronoun that includes the writer, the reader, and everybody else outside of the sugar plantation looking on in horror at the division of human beings into slaves and slave owners; we are so struck with horror that the blood leaves our bodies. There is also the problem of understanding why the negro in stanza one is "close to" rather than inside the sugar plantation, unless the phrase "junto al" simply acknowledges that the negro is the one closest to the production process. However, despite the ambivalence of the passage and the fact that the poem as a whole is anti-imperialistic, it is possible to claim that the Negro and the yanqui are united within the same spatial confines, inhabiting the same destiny. There is nowhere to stand except on the earth, and the earth is underneath the sugar plantation ("La tierra/bajo el cañaveral").

In a much later poem Guillén wrote as a tribute to Guatemala – a sister nation that has suffered just as much as Cuba – we find the lines: "¡Oh Guatemala con tu oscura herida!/¡Oh cuba, Oh patria con tu herida oscura!/ (Hay un sol que amanece en cada herida.)"[9] Despite the pain of the past, there seems to be hope; this hope does not come from the outside, but grows directly out of the wound.

In some of Guillén's late revolutionary poems, the inscription of sugar into *cubanidad* resurfaces as a key theme that is always treated critically but always accompanied by a recognition of the unavoidable role of sugar within the national imagination. One example is "Elegía a Jesus Menéndez," which was written in 1948 after the assassination of Jesús Menéndez, a close friend of Guillén and an important union leader in the sugar industry who acquired the nickname "The General of the Sugar Cane" (El General de la caña). The poem begins:

---

9   The poem was published in *La paloma de vuelo popular* in 1958. It is here quoted from Nicolás Guillén (1984), *El libro de los sonetos*, ed.Angel Augier, Habana: Ed. Unión, pp. 97-98. Eng. translation: "Oh, Guatemala with your dark wound!/ Oh Cuba, oh fatherland with your dark wound/ (There is a sun rising in each wound.)".

Las cañas iban y venían
Desesperadas, agitando
Las manos.
Te avisaban la muerte,[10]

Here the sugar canes become the allies of Mr. Menéndez, warning him about
the enemy. Lorna V. Williams has argued that the phrase "las manos" in this
poem, ostensibly referring to the "hands" of the sugar canes, might also refer
to the negro slaves since the metonymic fragmentation of black identity was
common in the sugar plantations, and black slaves were often referred to as
"manos" ("hands"; Williams 1982: 34-35). An intimate relation between, or
even identification of, the slaves and the canes is created. Later in the poem,
the sugar canes are heard speaking violently through the voice of the union
leader. After his assassination, the blood of Jesús Menéndez floods over his
assassinator, Joaquín Casillas, and later it washes over the exchange market
where it is sold at an extremely high price. A double meaning is implied here;
the blood of Jesús Menéndez is seen as very valuable at the economic market
but at the same time, the action of overflooding destroys the exchange market
and seems to undermine its logic.

Menéndez's murderer is caught in the sugar fields and the poem foresees
his approaching death. Casillas suffers a miserable death in moral degradation,
whereas Menéndez after his death becomes immortal. Guillén writes "¿Quién
vio caer a Jesús? Nadie lo viera, ni aun su asesino. Quedó en pie, rodeado de
cañas insurrectas, de cañas coléricas. Y ahora grita, resuena, no se detiene."[11]
The voice of Jesús mixes with the voices of the sugar canes and they rave at
Casillas:

Caña Mazanillo ejército
bala yanqui azúcar
crimen Manzanillo huelga
ingenio partido cárcel
dólar Manzanillo viuda

---

10   "Elegía a Jesús Menéndez" in *Las Grandes elegías*, 1984: 32ff. (English translation:
      "Elegy for Jesús Menéndez": "The sugar canes were restless,/desparate, waving/their
      hands/ they warned you about death,")

11   Ibid.: 38. English translation: "Who saw Jesús fall? Nobody saw him, not even his
      murderer. He stayed on his feet, surrounded by upright sugar canes, by choleric sugar
      canes. And now he shouts and sounds, he cannot be stopped."

entierro hijos padres
venganza Manzanillo zafra.[12]

Manzanillo, the place of the assassination, haunts the poem, but the name also recalls the rise of the independence movement, which was headed by Manuel de Céspedes from Manzanillo who in 1866 declared that the only purpose of society was "the independence of the Antilles and the absolute freedom of all its inhabitants, without regard to race or colour" (quoted in Ellis 1983,: 31). It is not easy to give a simple explanation of the passage from the poem, but it seems clear that the sugar canes want to avenge the death of Jesús Menéndez. They attack Casillas with words that are just as sharp as bullets or nails. In the final stanza in this complicated epic, Jesús Menéndez returns not as an avenging angel but as a smiling knight who carries with him "azúcar sin lágrimas" ("sugar without tears").

Many discourses are intermingled in this elegy: the religious discourse, which plays with the first name of Jesús Menéndez and installs him as a new Messiah; the economic discourse of the stock market; the political or ideological discourse; and a highly poetic, sonorous, and rhythmic discourse. The poem does not tell only one story but is rather constructed as an encounter between a number of different stories and discourses. Sugar plays an important role throughout, and not purely because it is closely related to the life of Jesús Menéndez; it becomes an active agent that will avenge his death and influence the future. In this sense, sugar becomes the poem's protagonist.

Guillén's elegy from 1948 for Jesús Menéndez anticipates the revolution: the voice of sugar is the voice of rebellion, of national liberation from inequality. In this way, sugar is interwoven with the destiny of the nation, dominating the most negative and the most positive developments in the country.

For El Cucalambé, the vision of national identity was an interweaving of Indian and white identities; in the poetry of Nicolás Guillén the national vision is negotiated between black and white identities or through mulato or *mestizo* identities. In both writers, a transcultural negotiation occurs which performatively writes a vision of the past, the present, and the future of the country. However, the poetry of Guillén fits more clearly into Ortiz's concept of the transcultural. In El Cucalambé, the national vision is harmonized

---

12   Ibid.: 38. English translation: "Sugar cane Manzanillo army/ bullet yankee sugar/crime Manzanillo strike/sugar mill party prison/dollar Manzanillo widow/funeral children parents/revenge Manzanillo sugar harvest".

without attention to the underlying fissures and conflicts, but this is not the case in Guillén. In his poetry, the whole painful process of acculturation, deculturation, and neoculturation becomes visible in different phases that all suffer losses, gaps, and deaths.

MODERNITY

In 19th-century Cuba, the sugar industry and the slave trade both grew rapidly while the civil rights of blacks deteriorated. At the same time, a new nationalism grew, not as *one* story about a true *cubanidad* but as multiple and very different stories of competing transcultural scenarios of development. In these scenarios, the subject of race invariably appears in very different forms. Our questions are: how does the issue of modernity appear within these different stories; and which story is the most modern? There are no simple answers to this.

In the 19th century, both the slave trade and the resistance movement could be said to be modern. The slave trade was modern in terms of the importation of machinery (for instance steam engines), the expansion of railway systems, and the urbanization process that it supported. Its economic logic was modern, and the rationalization of working processes and the instrumentalization of the work force were efficient and modern. The slave was not seen as a whole person with cultural roots but counted only in terms of his or her function in relation to the process of production. But the slave trade also built on power relations that were extremely conservative and in their lack of respect for human rights they seem quite anti-modern. On the other hand, part of the resistance movement, which saw itself as extremely modern and progressive and in accordance with enlightenment philosophy and liberal thinkers (for instance in the USA), was anti-modern in its desire for regression to an 'indigenous, original' Cuban culture free of the promiscuity of the modern sugar industry.

Perhaps it was not until after independence and the abolition of slavery were achieved that it became possible to understand the complexity of these processes. In the poetry of El Cucalambé, a new national unity is outlined which, in its blindness to potential conflicts, served as an important narrative in the independence war. According to the critic José Muñiz Vergara, *Los rumores del hórmigo* was quoted and used by the Separatist Party in particular. Guillén was writing in a different period, after independence had been established and the negative consequences of modernity had become more obvious.

A true modernity for Guillén is not simply material, superficial progress; it must also be conscious of the past, of previous circumstances that nevertheless live on as undercurrents in the new life. Blood is a recurring metaphor in the poetry of Guillén for this undercurrent, and sugar cane is his image for the rooting which will modify or qualify progress.

This is a key characteristic of the transcultural images of Nicolás Guillén: the past lives on, not through nostalgia but as a living reality that transforms the future. In "El apellido" ("The last name"), the "I" of the poem ponders both his roots and the "roots of his roots" ("las raíces de mis raíces") (*Las grandes elegías y otros poemas*: 18). He asks us if we really know him: "¿Tenéis todas mis señas? ¿Ya conocéis mi sangre navegable,/mi geografía llena de oscuros montes,/de hondos y amargos valles/ que no están en los mapas?" ("Do you have all my traits? Do you already know my navigatable blood/my geography full of dark hills,/of deep and bitter valleys/that do not exist in the maps?"). In the poem "Elegía cubana", Guillén warns us against forgetting, "Cuba, palmar vendido, sueño descuartizado,/duro mapa de azúcar y de olvido" ("Cuba, palm courts sold, splintered dream,/ hard map of sugar and forgetfulness")(*Las grandes elegías y otros poemas*: 14). If we forget, the present crystallizes and becomes hard and frozen; if we remember we partake in the living reality of the past within the present and the future, and this reality is always in Guillén of a transcultural character.

BIBLIOGRAPHY

Anderson, B. (1983). *Imagined Communities. Reflections on the Origin and Spread of Nationalism*. London, New York: Verso.

Benítez Rojo, A. (1986). Power/Sugar/Literature: Toward a reinterpretation of Cubanness. *Cuban Studies*, vol. 16, pp. 9-23.

Ellis, K. (1983). *Cuba's Nicolás Guillén. Poetry and Ideology*. Toronto/London: University of Toronto Press.

Fischer, S. (2004). *Modernity Disavowed. Haiti and the Cultures of Slavery in the Age of Revolution*. Durham: Duke University Press/University of West Indies Press.

Guillén, N. (1994). *Sóngoro cosongo. Poemas mulatos*. Habana: Ed. Unión.

Guillén, N. (1984). *El libro de los sonetos*. A. Augier, ed.. Habana: Ed. Unión.

Guillén, N. (1984). *Las grandes elegias y otros poemas*. A. Augier, ed.. Caracas: Biblioteca Ayacucho.

Lazo, R. (1974). *Historia de la literatura cubana*. México: Dirección General de Publicaciones.

Llorens, I. (1998). *Nacionalismo y literatura. Constitución e institucionalización de la "República de las letras cubanas"*. Lleida: Asociación Española de Estudios Literarios Hispanoamericanos.

Ortiz, F. (1940). *Contrapunteo cubano del tabaco y el azúcar*. E. M. Santí, ed.. Madrid: Cátedra Hispánica.

Ortiz, F. (2002). *Cuban Counterpoint*. Durham: Duke University Press.

Pérez, L. (1988). *Cuba Between Reform and Revolution*. Oxford: Oxford University Press.

Saco, J.A. (1832). Análisis por Don José Antonio Saco de una obra sobre el Brasil, intitulado, *Notices of Brazil in 1828 and 1829, by Rev. R. Walsh, Author of a Journey from Constantineople, etc.*", *Revistas Bimestre Cubana*. In Antonio Benítez Rojo (1986), p 21.

Staten, C.L. (2005). *The History of Cuba*. New York, Hampshire, England: Palgrave Macmillan.

Williams, L.V. (1982). *Self and Society in the Poetry of Nicolás Guillén*. Baltimore, London: Johns Hopkins University Press.

About the authors

Jim Mann, Professor, Ph.D., Human Nutrition and Medicine, University of Otago, Dunedin, New Zealand, Director of the Edgar National Centre for Diabetes and Obesity Research (ENCDOR) and the WHO Collaborating Centre for Human Nutrition. His research and clinical work have been primarily concerned with lipids and carbohydrates as they relate to coronary heart disease and diabetes, as well as the field of obesity. He has a particular interest in the concept of evidence-based nutrition and chairs the relevant International Union of Nutritional Science's (IUNS) working party. He is a principal investigator for the Riddet Institute, a national Centre of Research Excellence at Massey University, Palmerston North.

Recent Publications

Docherty, P., Berkeley, J., Lotz, T., Te Morenga, L., Fisk, L., Shaw, G.; McAuley, K., Mann, J., Chase, G (2012). Clinical validation of the quick dynamic insulin sensitivity test. *Biomedical Engineering, IEEE Transactions, pp.* (99), vol. 60, issue 5, 1, 0. doi: 10.1109/TBME.2012.2232667.

Te Morenga, L., Mallard, S., & Mann, J. (2013). Dietary sugars and body weight: Systematic review and meta-analyses of randomised controlled trials and cohort studies. *BMJ*, vol. 346, pp. 7492. doi: 10.1136/bmj.e7492

Brooking, L.A., Williams, S.M., & Mann, J.I. (2011). Effects of macronutrient composition of the diet on body fat in indigenous people at high risk of type 2 diabetes. *Diabetes Research & Clinical Practice. Advance online publication.* doi: 10.1016/j.diabres.2011.11.021

Per Bendix Jeppesen, Associate Professor, Ph.D., Department of Clinical Medicine, Diabetes Research Unit – Department of Medicine and Endocrinology (MEA), Aarhus University Hospital, Aarhus University. The Diabetes Research unit is an internationally renowned center for research on welfare diseases. Per Bendix Jeppesen is the leading expert in the research field regarding stevia, and has particular expertise in clinical human and animal studies on the effect of bioactive compounds on carbohydrate and lipid metabolism, prevention of diabetes, and insulin secretion using sophisticated molecular biological research methods. He is the coordinator and Faculty of Health representative for the newly established education in nutrition at Aarhus University

(Molecular Nutrition and Food Technology). Furthermore, he has international experience as the Clinical Management Leader for a DANIDA project in South America as well as research experience in both Japan and Brazil.

Recent Publications

Chen, X., Hermansen, K., Xiao, J., Bystrup, S.K., O'Driscoll, L., & Jeppesen, P.B. (2012). Isosteviol has beneficial effects on palmitate-induced α-cell dysfunction and gene expression. *PLoS One*, vol. 7, issue 3, pp. 34361.

Jeppesen, P.B. (2010). Isosteviol elevates plasma HDL-cholesterol level. In P.B. Jeppesen (Ed.). *Proceedings of the 4th Stevia symposium:* June 29 2010, KULeuven Belgium, pp. 173-189.

Ulla Kidmose, Associate Professor, Department of Food Science, Aarhus University. Ulla Kidmose has more than 20 years of research experience in food science. Her work is primarily within sensory science as well as the sensory and health qualities of plant-based food in relation to raw material, storage, processing, and preparation. As part of a large research project, her most recent focus has been on sensory interactions between different sweeteners and bitter tasting compounds. She has thorough competences in sensory analysis, using both a trained sensory panel as well as consumer preference tests.

Recent Publications

Bach, V., Kidmose, U., Bjørn, G.K., & Edelenbos, M. (2012). Effects of harvest time and variety on sensory quality and chemical composition of Jerusalem artichoke (Helianthus tuberosus) tubers. *Food Chemistry*, vol. 133, pp. 82-89.

Clausen, M.R. Pedersen, B.H., Bertram, H.C., & Kidmose, U. (2011). Quality of sour cherry juice of different clones and cultivars (Prunus cerasus L.) determined by a combined sensory and NMR spectroscopic approach. *Journal of Agricultural and food Chemistry*, vol. 59, pp. 12124-12130.

Heidi Kildegaard, Post-doctoral researcher, Department of Food Science, Aarhus University. Heidi Kildegaard has several years of experience researching sensory science and the nutritional qualities of food. Her Ph.D. thesis was about changing children's preferences toward healthier foods in a stepwise manner.

Recent Publications

Kildegaard, H., Tønning, E., and Thybo, A.T. (2011). Preference, liking and wanting for beverages in children aged 9-14 years: Roles of sourness perception, chemical composition and background variables. *Food Quality and Preference*, vol. 22, pp. 620-627.

Kildegaard, H. Løkke, M.M., & Thybo, A.T. (2011). Effect of increased fruit and fat content in an acified milk product on preference, liking and wanting. *Children. Journal of Sensory Studies*, vol 26, pp. 226-236.

Gitte K. Bjørn, MSc in Horticultural Science, AgroTech, Institute for Agri Technology and Food Innovation. Gitte Kjeldsen Bjørn has more than 20 years of research experience in plant food production. Her main research area is within cultivars of vegetables, including issues of yield, quality, disease, and nutritional aspects.

Recent Publications

Bach, V., Kidmose, U., Bjørn, G.K., & Edelenbos, M. (2012). Effects of harvest time and variety on sensory quality and chemical composition of Jerusalem artichoke (Helianthus tuberosus) tubers. *Food Chemistry*, vol 133, pp. 82-89.

Dresbøll, D., Bjørn, G.K., Thorup-Kristensen, K. (2008). Yields and the extent and causes of damage in cauliflower, bulb onion, and carrot grown under organic or conventional regimes. *Journal of Horticultural Science & Biotechnology*, vol 83, issue 6, pp. 770-776.

Susanne Højlund, Associate Professor, Ph.D., Anthropology, Department of Culture and Society Aarhus University. Her research covers topics such as welfare, childhood, youth, institutional ethnography, the concept of home, and food. She is currently working on different projects related to the cultural study of food, including sugar policy in children's institutions, cultural borders between edible and non-edible food, and the social aesthetics of tasting.

Recent Publications

Dalsgård, A.L., Frederiksen, M. D., Højlund, S.; Meinert, L, (Eds.). (forthcoming 2014). *Ethnographies of Youth and Temporality: Time Objectified*. Temple University Press.

Højlund, S., Langer, S. (Eds). (2011). Foreword. An anthropology of welfare: Journeying towards the good life. *Anthropology in Action*, vol. 18, issue 3, pp. 1-9.

Højlund, S. (2011). Home as a model for sociality in Danish children's homes: A question of authenticity. *Social Analysis*, vol. 55, issue 2, pp. 106-120.

Ken Henriksen, Associate Professor, Ph.D., Latin American Studies, Department of Aesthetics and Communication, Aarhus University. His main interests are modernization and democratization, ethnicity, citizenship, and human rights. In recent years he has also researched globalization and Latin American immigration to the U.S. He is principal editor of the journal *Diálogos Latinoamericanos*.

Recent publications

Henriksen, K. (2012). Positioning Latinos/as between exclusion and transnational spaces. *American Studies in Scandinavia*, vol. 43, issue 1, pp. 3-15.

Henriksen, K., & Kindblad, C. (2011). Neoliberalism, patriarchal rule, and cultural change at the turn of the twentieth century. The case of Tasbapauni. In Baracco, L. (Ed.) (2011). *National Integration and Contested Autonomy: The Caribbean Coast of Nicaragua*. New York: Algora Publishing, pp. 191-219.

Henriksen, K.(2010). The external creation of Latino Others. Online discussion communities and Latino cultural citizenship in San Diego, USA. *FIAR: Forum for Inter-American Research*, vol. 3, issue 1, http://www.interamerica.de/volume-3-1/henriksen/

Anne Oehlerich, Anthropologist MSc, South America Coordinator for the Swedish NGO "Solaridad Suecia America Latina," Santa Cruz, Bolivia. External lecturer, Department of Anthropology and Ethnography, Aarhus University. She has written a master's thesis on traditional medicine, illness, and disease perceptions, and has worked with institutional capacity building of indigenous movements in Bolivia and Peru since 1995. She is a designer and consultant for exhibitions about the Guarani Indigenous People in Bolivia and for the Unesco Collection about Quechua and Aymara Indians, Moesgaard Museum, Aarhus, Denmark.

Vinicius Mariano de Carvalho, Associate Professor, Ph.D., Brazilian Studies, Department of Aesthetics and Communication, Aarhus University. He is a member of the Research Group Sugar and Modernity in Latin America, in which he develops research on José Lins do Rego's literary works (the sugar cane cycle). He has lectured on this research at Universities in Brazil (Rio de Janeiro, Juiz de Fora, Salvador) and England (King's College London), as well at his own university in Denmark. He also presented his research at the Anthropos conference in Cuba in 2011, together with the research group.

Recent publications

Carvalho, V.M. de (2013). Verflechtungen und Entflechtungen. In S. Klengel, C. Quandt, P. W. Schulze, & G. Wink (Eds.). *Desde que o Samba é Samba* von Paulo Lins. *Novas vozes. Zur brasilianischen Literatur im 21. Jahrhundert*. Frankfurt: Vervuert Verlag, pp. 125-146

Carvalho, V.M. de (2011). Democracia directa en America Latina: Introducción a la sección temática. In V.M. Carvalho & J.G.G. Chourio (Eds.). *Dialogos Latinoamericanos*, vol 18, issue 5.

Karen-Margrethe Simonsen, Associate Professor, Ph.D., Comparative Literature, Department of Aesthetics and Communication, Aarhus University, Director of the research group "Humanistic Studies of Human Rights," Aarhus University. Her research is centred on law and literature, human rights, and transnational literary historiography. Currently she is working on a project about the development of human rights after the discovery of the new world in a transatlantic perspective. She focuses on the parallel development of human rights in Europe and slavery in the sugar plantations in the Caribbean, as well as how sugar becomes an 'engine' for modernity and a metaphor for transcultural exchange. She is editor of the journal *K&K. Kultur og Klasse.*

Recent publications

Simonsen, K. (forthcoming 2013). The politics of universalism. Strategic uses of human rights discourses in early modernity. *Journal of Aesthetics and Culture.*

Simonsen, K. (Ed.) (2013). *Law and Justice in Literature, Film and Theatre. Nordic Perspectives on Law and Humanities*. Law and Literature 5. Berlin/New York: Walter De Gruyter. Info: http://www.degruyter.com/view/product/184907